Professional Development
for Culturally Responsive
and Relationship-Based Pedagogy

To Cheri
Christie Sleeter
Nov-13, 2012

Rochelle Brock and Richard Greggory Johnson III
Executive Editors

Vol. 24

The Black Studies and Critical Thinking series
is part of the Peter Lang Education list.
Every volume is peer reviewed and meets
the highest quality standards for content and production.

PETER LANG
New York • Washington, D.C./Baltimore • Bern
Frankfurt • Berlin • Brussels • Vienna • Oxford

Professional Development for Culturally Responsive and Relationship-Based Pedagogy

Edited by Christine E. Sleeter

PETER LANG
New York • Washington, D.C./Baltimore • Bern
Frankfurt • Berlin • Brussels • Vienna • Oxford

Library of Congress Cataloging-in-Publication Data

Professional development for culturally responsive and relationship-based pedagogy /
edited by Christine E. Sleeter.
p. cm. — (Black studies and critical thinking ; v. 24)
Includes bibliographical references and index.
1. Multicultural education—Cross-cultural studies. 2. Minorities—Education—
Cross-cultural studies. 3. Teachers—Training of—Cross-cultural studies.
4. Education—Social aspects—Cross-cultural studies.
5. Critical pedagogy—Cross-cultural studies. I. Sleeter, Christine E.
LC1099.P754 370.117—dc23 2011033355
ISBN 978-1-4331-1471-7 (hardcover)
ISBN 978-1-4331-1470-0 (paperback)
ISBN 978-1-4539-0206-6 (e-book)
ISSN 1947-5985

Bibliographic information published by **Die Deutsche Nationalbibliothek**.
Die Deutsche Nationalbibliothek lists this publication in the "Deutsche
Nationalbibliografie"; detailed bibliographic data is available
on the Internet at http://dnb.d-nb.de/.

This research was supported in part by Contract No. 387-2904
awarded to Victoria University and by Contract No. 387-1544 awarded
to the University of Waikato by the New Zealand Ministry of Education.
The opinions expressed here, however, are those of the authors
and do not necessarily reflect those of the Ministry of Education,
and no official endorsement should be inferred.

Cover art by Hare Te Pura Te Rangiamo Pitama | Iwi: Kai Tahu
Painting: Tino Rangatiratanga verses Kawanatanga
Series: 1 of 2 both held in private collections
Email: hpitama@xtra.co.nz

The paper in this book meets the guidelines for permanence and durability
of the Committee on Production Guidelines for Book Longevity
of the Council of Library Resources.

CONTENTS

· 1 ·

THE QUEST FOR SOCIAL JUSTICE IN THE EDUCATION OF MINORITIZED STUDENTS

Christine Sleeter, California State University Monterey Bay

A pressing problem facing nations around the world today is the persistence of educational disparities that adversely affect minoritized students, and by extension, the nation as a whole. As Shields, Bishop and Mazawi (2005) explain, the term "minoritized" refers to those who, while not necessarily in the numerical minority, have been ascribed characteristics of a minority and are treated as if their position and perspective is of less worth. Exactly who are the minoritized students varies somewhat from country to country, but they generally include Indigenous students, students of color, students whose families live in poverty, and new immigrants whose parents have relatively low levels of schooling. As populations of minoritized students expand, the urgency of addressing disparities increases.

For example, in the United States, one can see the future population mix in the current school-age population, which is more racially, ethnically, and linguistically diverse than ever due to higher birth rates among communities of color, who tend to be younger than the White population, and net immigration of minoritized peoples. In 2008, students were 58% White, 22% Hispanic, 16% Black, 4% Asian and Pacific Islander, and 1% Native American (U.S. Department of Education, 2010). Yet, this growing proportion of students continues to experience disparities in school achievement from early childhood through university level. Villegas and Lucas (2002) noted that "[h]istorically, members of economically poor and minority groups have not succeeded in schools at rates comparable to those of their white, middle-class, standard English-speaking peers" (p. xi). As one snapshot indicator, according to Aud, Fox, and KewalRamani (2010), White, African American, and Asian 4-year-olds demonstrated higher rates of proficiency in letter recognition than Latino and American Indian 4-year-olds in a 2005 comparison. In reading, on the 2007 National Assessment of Educational Progress assessment, higher percentages of Asian/Pacific Islander and White 4th- and 8th-graders scored at or above Proficient than did African American, Latino, or American Indian students at the same grade levels, as did a higher percentage of White than non-White 12th graders. In mathematics, on the 2005 and 2009 National Assessment of Educational Progress assessment, higher percentages of Asian/Pacific Islander students in 4th, 8th, and 12th grades scored at or above Proficient than did White, Black, Latino, and American Indian students at the same grade levels. On the Scholastic Aptitude Test for entry into university, White students had the highest average critical reading score in 2008 and Asian students had the highest average mathematics score.

Similar disparities are evident in New Zealand schools. In 2010, students were 55% New Zealand European, 22% Indigenous Māori, 10% Pacific Nations, and 10% Asian immigrant and other (Ministry of Education, 2010). In mainstream schools Māori students are overrepresented in special education programs, leave school early with fewer qualifications, and are overrepresented in school expulsion and suspension figures compared with the dominant New Zealand European students (Ministry of Education, 2006). One finds the same picture with respect to Aboriginal students in Canada (Cherubini, Hodson, Manley-Casimir & Muir, 2010; Kanu, 2007), and in Australia, where in 2002 the 38% retention rate for Indigenous students contrasted sharply with a 76% retention rate for non-Indigenous students (Moyle, 2005). In India, rapidly expanded access to schooling has resulted in schools having much more diverse populations in terms of language, caste, gender, family income, and religion. At the same time, disparities in educational attainment are sharp (Kumar, 2010).

In Europe, particularly "old Member states" of the European Union, migrations of people from previous colonies and other sending countries, with their different age structures and birth rates, have expanded the diversity of its school-age population. Now sizable groups of ethnic and religious minorities are evident in most towns and cities (Luciak, 2006). As Liégeois (2007) put it, "The convergence of these two phenomena, migration and the emergence of minorities, has reconfigured the demographic, social, cultural, and European political landscape, a landscape now marked by pluriculturalism or multiculturalism" (p. 12). This pattern of increasing diversity is coupled with persistent and increasing educational disparities, primarily between those from dominant cultural groups as well as relatively well-educated immigrants (Holdaway, Crul & Roberts, 2009), and those of minoritized children, which include African Caribbeans, Roma, Travellers in Ireland, and Muslims in Greece (Luciak, 2006). For example, in Britain, despite fluctuations in the magnitude of the gap in various indicators of school achievement between White and African Caribbean Black students, the gap itself remains constant (Gillborn, 2008).

The situation of increasingly diverse student populations being taught by persistently non-diverse teaching forces exacerbates the problem of disparities in achievement. For example, in the U.S. in 2008, while about 58% of the students were White, about 82% of public school teachers were White, proportions that had not changed markedly over the years (U.S. Department of Education, 2010). In New Zealand, while 55% of the students identify as New Zealand European, 74% of teachers do so while only 9% of teachers identify as Māori, 3% as Pasifika, and 14% as other (Ministry of Education, 2010). In Canada, the growing numbers of Aboriginal children in classrooms are being taught largely by non-Aboriginal teachers who generally lack the background and training to teach them well (Cherubini, Hodson, Manley-Casimir & Muir, 2010). Teachers with a limited range of cross-cultural experiences and understandings are often unaware of the "funds of knowledge" that children of different backgrounds can call upon in classrooms, and may not understand the cultural cues that people use to indicate their willingness to enter into dialogue fundamental to learning (Gay, 2010; Gonzalez, Moll & Amanti, 2005). As a result, one commonly finds teachers using pedagogical practices and models of education more appropriate to the dominant populations than to the diverse populations in their classrooms, drawing on deficit discourses when these do not work (Bishop, 2005).

Common Approaches to Understanding and Addressing Disparities

Because of the urgent need to address educational disparities, countries, states, provinces, and cities commonly have plans in place, at least at the level of policy documents. For example, the legislation known as *No Child Left Behind* in the U.S. announces this goal prominently. In the United Kingdom, speaking to the DfE Single Equality Scheme, Secretary of State for Education Michael Gove proclaimed that, "Raising standards and narrowing gaps are the central goals of the government's education policy" (Department for Education, 2010). The Hon. Julia Gillard MP, formerly Minister for Education, Minister for Employment and Workplace Relations, and Minister for Social Inclusion, now Prime Minister of Australia, announced policy commitment to "Closing the gap between Indigenous and non-Indigenous Australians" (Gillard, 2008). Indian Prime Minister Manmohan Singh stated in 2009 that, "The role of education is to uphold equity and tolerance . . . these are all-important in a country like ours which has diversities, to emerge as a strong nation" (Kumar, 2010, p. 41).

Yet, the successes of such plans are generally underwhelming. In the U.S., for example, although newspaper announcements often tout achievement gaps that are being closed as a result of *No Child Left Behind*, careful perusal of student achievement data does not warrant enthusiasm (Ravitch, 2010). Below three approaches to understanding and addressing disparities are reviewed. I will argue that deficit-oriented approaches, while the most common, are least helpful, while emancipatory approaches that include culturally responsive pedagogy, while least common, have the most power to bring about lasting change.

Deficit-oriented approaches

Deficit-oriented approaches to understanding and addressing disparities, though inherently problematic, continue to be very common. For example, in a discussion of the persistent racial disparities in U.S. education, Noguera (2002) noted that the most commonly-held explanations evaluate presumed cultural characteristics of racial and ethnic groups: "it is widely believed that Asian-American students do well academically because they come from a culture that emphasizes the importance of hard work and the pursuit of academic excellence. . . . In contrast, African-American and Latino students are perceived as being held back by attitudes of opposition and a culture of poverty" (p. 6). Similarly, writing about Indian teachers' beliefs, Kumar (2010) pointed out that teachers commonly connect children's ascribed identities with assumptions about their educability that teachers regard as rooted in the parents' level of schooling.

Deficit-oriented perspectives find data-based support in surveys that correlate student achievement with student background factors without examining school processes. For example, in a large-scale survey of factors that correlate with reading achievement in 30 countries, Marks, Cresswell and Ainley (2006) found that cultural resources operationalized as books in the home and possession of classic literature and art explained more of the variance in student reading achievement than did family economic resources or several school factors. However, missing from the study was information about classroom pedagogy, teacher expectations, and the extent to which schools capitalize on non-mainstream cultural resources students do have.

The 'solution' from a deficit perspective, is to 'free' students from 'pathological' cultures of their homes by helping them to acquire more of the dominant culture. Writing about Māori education in New Zealand, Penetito (2010) remarked that,

> The mainstream system has always accepted Māori students, but it has consistently treated them paternalistically. . . . For Māori, the message has always been: to achieve comparability in any aspect of the education system, you are to set aside your Māoritanga (qualities that distinguish you as a Māori) in favor of acquiring Pāketātanga (qualities that demonstrate your socialization into Pākehā).[1] (p. 15)

Compensatory education has been the main deficit-oriented solution to disparities. It has taken a variety of forms, ranging from remedial basic skills education (Woolfolk, 2001), to transition bilingual programs that aim to move students into the dominant language as quickly as possible (Billings, Martin-Beltran & Hernandez, 2010), to offering minoritized students supplementary schooling so they can catch up. In a critique of deficit-oriented approaches to working with immigrant students in Spain, Rodríguez Izquierdo (2009) noted that such is manifest in:

> la concepción de la educación compensatoria como dispositivo para adecuar a los niños al ritmo de la clase, en la utilización de métodos de tratamiento de los trastornos del lenguaje para la enseñanza del castellano como segunda lengua, en la reducción de la diversidad a problema lingüístico.
>
> [the concept of compensatory education as a device to bring children into the rhythm of the classroom, the use of methods of treating disorders of language for teaching Castilian as a second language to reduce the diversity of the language problems.]

While compensatory education rests on problematic assumptions about minoritized communities that ignore systemic racism, and many such programs do not in fact improve students' learning (e.g., Rodríguez Izquierdo, 2009), some do produce small achievement gains. For example, in the U.S., Head Start provides a range of services to preschool children and their parents that more affluent families already have access to. Although evaluation studies of the impact of Head Start have been mixed, partly because of the varied quality of programs, they tend to find modest positive gains for children who have participated in Head Start in comparison to those who have not (Jung & Stone, 2008; Nathan, 2007). As another example, Title I authorizes funds to states and local educational agencies that have high concentrations of children in poverty to provide supplemental remedial education services. The initial intent was to enable schools to close the achievement gap between children in poverty and children from more affluent communities. Early evaluations found most Title I interventions to be largely ineffective. However, due to revisions in the nature of programs that qualify, they have become somewhat more effective in boosting the achievement of children in poverty (Borman, 2005).

Although minoritized communities critique and often reject deficit-oriented approaches because of their inherent devaluing of family and community cultures (e.g., Penetito, 2010; Yosso, 2005), such approaches refuse to go away. This is so probably because of the small successes of some compensatory programs, but even more because such approaches suggest that dominant communities have no culpability for the existence of disparities. In fact, educators from dominant groups often deny the deficit orientation within their own deficit explanations for disparities. The current popularity of Ruby Payne in U.S. schools is an example. Payne is an entrepreneur who consults with schools about how to teach children in poverty. Her message is largely one of offering strategies teachers can use to help children in poverty acquire aspects of middle class culture. Payne (2009) argues that her approach is not deficit-oriented because it focuses on how to help children escape the culture of poverty.

In a critique of Payne's message to educators, however, Bomer, Dworin, May and Semingson (2009) pinpoint several central problems with deficit-oriented approaches that arise from a failure to acknowledge the cultural resources children and their families have, and the way discrimination becomes institutionalized when programs and practices are built around that failure:

> Deficit perspectives, when educators hold them, have been shown in much research to lower the quality of education for children from low-income households (see e.g., Ansalone, 2003; Anyon, 1980; Connor & Boskin, 2001; Dudley-Marling, 2007; Gamoran & Berends, 1987; Moll, 1988; Moll & Ruiz, 2002; Oakes, 1985; Rist, 1970; Valenzuela, 1999). The kinds of conversations available to them are diminished, the

scope of the curriculum contracts, the modalities in which they are asked to represent their learning are constricted.

And yet, deficit orientations persist as dominant groups attempt to maintain control over the education system into which minoritized students might assimilate. As Penetito (2010) argued with reference to Māori education in New Zealand, the mainstream system has always selected and filtered which aspects of Māori culture are admissible into the schooling system. Deficit thinking, then, normalized in the minds of many educators and in the routinized ways schooling is done, is bound up with the politics of who gets to exercise control.

Structural approaches

Structural approaches to understanding and addressing disparities focus on equalizing student access to inequitably distributed resources, such as high quality programs or teachers (e.g., Haycock & Hanushek, 2010). Rather than viewing the home and community culture of students as the main source of disparities, structural approaches look to systems in which students are educated.

For example, in a comprehensive study of the underachievement of English language learners in California (the great majority of whom speak Spanish as their first language), Gándara, Rumberger, Maxwell-Jolly and Callahan (2003) identified the following specific inequitable structures that place English learners at a disadvantage: access to qualified teachers and to teachers who are trained to teach English learners, access to good instructional materials and schooling conditions, meaningful assessment that identifies what students actually know rather than what they can communicate in English, access to rigorous coursework and to school counselors, time in classrooms that is used specifically for instruction, and segregation of English learners. They argued that all of these forms of inequitable resource distribution can be addressed, and that doing so would meaningfully address disparities in student learning. Similarly, in a "parsing" of the achievement gap in the U.S., Barton and Coley (2009) examined 16 inequitable conditions for learning for students of color and for students from low-income families. School conditions included access to the following: an academically rigorous curriculum, qualified and experienced teachers, lower class sizes, instructional technology, and a safe learning environment. The study also examined home and community factors such as exposure to environmental toxins and time spent viewing television. The authors argued that achieving equitable conditions of learning would substantially narrow achievement gaps; they also noted that inequitable conditions have deep roots that require a broad and comprehensive set of policies to address.

Similar kinds of structural barriers in schools have been identified in countries around the world. For example, Luciak (2006) describes segregation of minoritized students in many European countries, where they tend to be placed in "schools that are less academically challenging and of shorter duration," and in which students are "overrepresented in special education" (p. 76). In England, school processes of "selection and separation" support racism, particularly "setting" pupils into hierarchical "ability" groups, creating pathways for "gifted and talented" students, and creating specialist schools. In this system, which purports to be colorblind, Black Caribbean students end up with disproportionately less access to academically advanced curricula and teaching than White students and Indian immigrants (Gillborn, 2007).

Unlike a deficit orientation to understanding the underachievement of minoritized students, a structural analysis points toward systemic changes that could be made, such as reducing or eliminating tracking/streaming, ensuring that students who need excellent teachers the most get them, ensuring that all students have access to an academically challenging curriculum, reducing or eliminating segregation, ensuring that assessment systems are culturally fair, and so forth. Many current school reforms do, in fact, explicitly focus on some of these structural inequities, particularly access to a challenging academic curriculum.

For example, a prominent model in the U.S. is a system of charter schools known as the Knowledge Is Power Program (KIPP). KIPP's mission is to prepare minoritized students for university, and its schools are experiencing high rates of success in closing achievement gaps. Based on a study of three KIPP schools, Macey, Decker and Eckes (2009) synthesized the connected strategies that appear to contribute to KIPP schools' success. Strategies that address structural issues include ensuring students access to a rigorous college preparatory curriculum that is taught by teachers who are hired for their dedication, many of whom graduated from prestigious institutions; increased instructional time (a longer school day, school every other Saturday, and summer school); and consistency of expectations, rewards and sanctions across classrooms. Other factors include hiring relatively young, enthusiastic teachers and principals who are dedicated to the mission of KIPP and willing to do whatever is needed to close the achievement gap (significantly, almost half of the teachers were of color), and hiring instructional coaches who observe teachers and offer them feedback and help regularly. These important additional factors suggest limitations of a structural analysis alone, as they indicate the importance of culture as well as of how teachers position themselves toward their students and students' families.

No Child Left Behind addresses disparities by focusing on a selection of structural factors, particularly access to a rigorous curriculum, then legislating that schools must bring all students up to the same achievement standards. But it ignores other significant structural factors such the institutionalization of poverty (Anyon, 2005; Berliner, 2006). And, while ostensibly rejecting a cultural deficiency approach, spotlighting achievement disparities without offering a very deep analysis of why they exist, coupled with implying that treating the growing diversity of students as if they were identical will reduce disparities, fails to counter deficit thinking when disparities remain.

Emancipatory approaches

Emancipatory approaches to understanding and addressing disparities locate both how the problem is defined and why it continues to exist in unequal power relationships in schools as well as the broader society. From an emancipatory perspective, disparities exist because schools are institutionalized to produce them, through practices such as assigning students to schools based on race and class segregated residential patterns, staffing schools mainly with members of the dominant society, structuring curriculum and assessment around the knowledge and worldview of the dominant group, and classifying and streaming students based on their mastery of this curriculum. While confronting structural disparities, emancipatory approaches begin with the premise that those who experience disparities know best what the problems are, thus shifting who defines the problems and their solutions from members of the dominant society to marginalized communities, as part of a broader effort to claim, share, and use power for the community's benefit.

Within contexts that the dominant society controls, even when that control seems benevolent, children and youth from minoritized communities internalize deficit perspectives about themselves and their communities, which impacts negatively not only on their school achievement but also on their mental health. Research studies investigating students of color in different regions of the U.S., for example, have consistently found a relationship between academic achievement, level of awareness of race and racism, and identification with students' own racial group. Students who have a strong ethnic identity and are aware of barriers of discrimination are likely to see education as a tool of liberation, thereby taking it seriously (Altschul, Oyserman & Bybee, 2006; Chavous et al., 2003; Miller & MacIntosh, 1999; Sanders, 1997). For example, Altschul, Oyserman and Bybee (2008) surveyed 185 Latino/a 8th graders in 3 low-income middle schools where students ranged from being recent immigrants to second- and third-generation; most were of Mexican descent. Students with higher grades tended to have bicultural identities, identifying with their ethnic origin as well as focusing on overcoming obstacles within mainstream society. Students who identified little with their ethnic origin tended to achieve poorly, as did the relatively fewer students who identified exclusively with their culture of origin and not at all with the mainstream society. Based on in-depth interviews with high-achieving African American adolescents, Carter (2008) and O'Connor (1997) found that having a critical consciousness of race and racism and a strong Black identity helped the students develop an achievement ideology and a sense of agency.

Emancipatory knowledge counters perspectives generated by dominant social groups. For example, in addition to common use of cultural deficiency explanations, mainstream explanations of the underachievement of minoritized students are often couched in terms of psychological factors such as motivation or self-perception of competence (e.g., Pershey, 2010). While such analyses may suggest school interventions, they still tend to locate the problem within the student. Conversely, work such as Ladson-Billings's (1995) study of successful teachers of African American children, which was generated within the African American community, interpreted through African American professional thought, and explicitly designed to improve teaching of African American children, focused on classroom pedagogy that made a difference. In generating a vision of culturally relevant pedagogy, Ladson-Billings and the teachers placed culture and analysis of political oppression at the fore, constructing teaching as a tool of intellectual liberation, a vision that has long been common among African American educators (e.g., Woodson, 1933). Significantly, culturally relevant pedagogy describes what teachers do with minoritized students that both produces academic success as well as validating who they are. Similarly, writing with regard to the limits of conventional approaches to addressing the academic underachievement of Māori students, Penetito (2010) argued that Māori do have "remedies for this problem," but that "the system has continually set out to address the problem of disparity between Māori and non-Māori academic performance rather than explain the marginalization of Māori knowledge, history, and custom within the system" (p. 58). In other words, the dominant society tries to maintain control by addressing minoritized students' underachievement itself, rather than turning to and learning directly from minoritized communities.

Several somewhat different but related theoretical strands and practices can be considered emancipatory approaches. Critical race theory, for example, which emerged in the U.S. during the early 1980s as scholars of color in legal studies began to examine the intransigence of racism following the civil rights movement and the role of the law in maintaining unequal race relations, serves as a counter to analyses of diversity and disparity that do not specifically examine race and power (Dixson & Rousseau, 2006; Ladson-Billings & Tate, 1995; Solórzano & Delgado Bernal, 2001). Its main goal is to expose hidden systemic and customary ways in which racism works, drawing from a wide variety of sources ranging from statistics to social science research to personal experience. While much initial work in critical race theory was articulated largely within a Black/White binary, scholars of color have found the focus on racism immensely helpful, and many have adapted it to the histories, experiences, and concerns of specific communities of color. For example, developing TribalCrit theory with respect to American Indian tribes, Brayboy (2005) points out that for Indigenous peoples, colonialism is more fundamental than race. He argues that TribalCrit scholars "must expose structural inequalities and assimilatory processes and work toward debunking and deconstructing them" as well as working "to create structures that will address the real, immediate and future needs of tribal peoples and communities" (p. 440). He emphasizes that the entire process of both exposing the roots of disparities as well as addressing them must be conducted "with Indigenous Peoples" rather than "for" them (p. 440).

In New Zealand, Kaupapa Māori theory, research, and approaches to schooling emerged during the 1980s as a process through which Māori name the world, its problems, and their solutions (Bishop, 2003; Fitzsimons & Smith, 2000). According to Penetito (2010), "the kaupapa Māori agenda is about both the reproduction of Māori culture through schooling and the transformation of dominant structures within the broader context of education" (p. 225). Schools (kura) based on a Kaupapa Māori orientation have greatly expanded over the past 20 years, having a transformative impact on thousands of Māori students. As Penetito explains, reproduction of Māori culture does not mean returning to the culture of a century ago, but rather the power of Māori today to define their own goals and processes for achieving those goals.

While emancipatory approaches to addressing disparities focus on a wide range of power relations, there is a clear emphasis on classroom pedagogy that values students' cultural communities and that directly addresses the conditions of oppression their communities face. Critical pedagogy and culturally responsive pedagogy are forms of emancipatory pedagogy that relate to this book.

Critical and culturally responsive pedagogy

Freire (1972, 1973, 1976) argued throughout his life that oppressed people must develop a critical consciousness that will enable denouncing dehumanizing social structures, and announcing social transformation. In the process of teaching literacy to adults, he created a process of culture circles in which students took up topics of concern to them, discussed and debated them in order to clarify and develop their thinking, and developed strategies for acting on their concerns. A fundamental task in culture circles was to distinguish between what humans have created and what nature created, in order to identify what role humans can play in bringing about social change. Freire's connection between critical education and political work for liberation became an important basis for critical pedagogy.

Critical pedagogy engages students to analyze inequities in their own lives and advocate for justice. Duncan-Andrade and Morrell (2008), for example, explain that in their own secondary school teaching, while critical pedagogy did not preclude them from using traditional canonical texts, and it definitely involved teaching to very high academic expectations, critical pedagogy also meant using practices that were "explicitly aware of issues of power, oppression, and transformation, that honored the non-school cultural practices of the students, and that included the students in authentic dialogue about inequity and advocacy for justice" (p. 51). Their teaching tapped into students' everyday life experiences and deep familiarity with popular culture "to scaffold academic literacies" (p. 54), while simultaneously helping students learn to read and act on the world politically.

Similarly, culturally responsive pedagogy situates teaching and learning within an analysis of oppression. Gay (2010) defines culturally responsive pedagogy as teaching "to and through [students'] personal and cultural strengths, their intellectual capabilities, and their prior accomplishments"

(p. 26); culturally responsive pedagogy is premised on "close interactions among ethnic identity, cultural background, and student achievement" (p. 27). Ladson-Billings (1995) proposed three dimensions of culturally relevant pedagogy: holding high academic expectations and offering appropriate support such as scaffolding; acting on cultural competence by reshaping curriculum, building on students' funds of knowledge, and establishing relationships with students and their homes; and cultivating students' critical consciousness regarding power relations. While these definitions overlap, they are not identical: Ladson-Billings' conception includes critical pedagogy in its emphasis on developing students' critical consciousness, while Gay's conception focuses more strongly on culture. In an attempt to operationalize culturally relevant pedagogy as reflected in 45 classroom-based studies of teacher practice, Morrison, Robbins and Rose (2008) found 12 kinds of actions that they classified into three broad categories, following Ladson-Billings's (1995) theoretical framework. Significantly, none of the 45 studies depicted all 12 key actions, although each study depicted several of them. Nonetheless, there was agreement that culturally responsive pedagogy, however it is specifically defined, is a significant emancipatory approach to addressing disparities.

Research on the impact of culturally responsive pedagogy on student outcomes, however, is rather thin, consisting mainly of case studies, program descriptions, and anecdotes (Brayboy & Castango, 2009; Gay, 2010). Many studies illustrate what it looks like in practice, although most of these do not report student outcome data (e.g., Cazden, 1989; Duncan-Andrade, 2007; Ladson-Billings, 1994; Lee, 2001; Matthews, 2003; Sleeter & Stillman, 2007). There are case studies that connect culturally responsive pedagogy with student engagement, suggesting that academic learning follows from engagement (e.g., Hill, 2009; Howard, 2001; Nykiel-Herbert, 2010). Several promising projects demonstrate positive impact on students, including the Algebra Project and the Kamehameha Early Elementary Project for Native Hawaiians (see Gay, 2010 for a detailed review).

Only a few projects that currently exist embody a robust conceptualization of culturally responsive pedagogy, and have produced published data demonstrating their impact on student outcomes, including achievement. Math in a Cultural Context (MCC) connects Yup'ik Alaska Native culture and knowledge with mathematics as outlined in the National Council of Teachers of Mathematics standards. The project was developed through collaboration between math educators, Yup'ik teachers, and Yup'ik elders. A few small-scale experimental studies report that students in classrooms using MCC make more progress toward the state mathematics standards than students in classrooms not using it (Lipka & Adams, 2004; Lipka et al., 2005).

Lee's (2006) Cultural Modeling project "is a framework for the design of curriculum and learning environments that links everyday knowledge with learning academic subject matter, with a particular focus on racial/ethnic minority groups, especially youth of African descent" (p. 308). Lee posits that African American life affords young people a wealth of cultural scripts and contexts that can be used in the classroom to develop literary analysis strategies students can then apply to unfamiliar texts, and that pedagogy that enables students to use their cultural frames of reference immediately engages them in much higher levels of cognition than is usually the case with a traditional curriculum. Lee's small-scale studies find that African American students learn literary analysis better through this culturally responsive pedagogical strategy than through traditional teaching (Lee, 1995, 2001, 2006).

Cammarota and Romero (2009) report data on the impact of the Social Justice Education Project on secondary Chicano students in high poverty schools in Tucson, Arizona. Their model of "critically conscious intellectualism" has three components: (1) curriculum that is culturally and historically relevant to the Chicano students, focuses on social justice issues, and is academically rigorous; (2) critical pedagogy in which students develop critical consciousness by gathering data on a problem involving racism in their own community and analyzing the problem using social science theoretical frameworks, and (3) authentic caring in which teachers demonstrate deep respect for students as intellectual and full human beings. The authors have documented a direct connection between student participation in the program and subsequent academic achievement on the state basic skills test, as well as high school graduation and subsequent university entrance.

As these examples show, culturally responsive pedagogy is promising. Based on their review projects such as these, Brayboy and Castagno (2009) note that,

> There are a number of examples in the literature of programs that have successfully developed and implemented CRS [culturally responsive schooling] for Indigenous youth. What many of these case studies have in common is a 'grass roots' approach in which local communities play a key role in developing and sustaining the program, sustained financial support, and careful record-keeping of both achievements and setbacks. (p. 45)

The project that is the subject of this book—Te Kotahitanga—focuses on helping teachers shift the nature of pedagogy in their classrooms in a way that enables minoritized students to participate and learn. In subsequent chapters, we not only show what the implementation of culturally responsive pedagogy looks like in classrooms, but also link its use with student outcome data. We fully recognize that this focus on classroom pedagogy addresses one significant layer of a much larger system of institutionalized disparities and control. However, for students, what happens in the classroom is central.

Teacher Professional Development

This book takes up the question of how teachers can be supported in learning to work with culturally responsive pedagogy, given the cultural, experiential, and social gaps between the majority of teachers and minoritized students. Ideally an emancipatory approach would staff schools with teachers who bring a critical consciousness and a keen understanding of students' lives and cultural backgrounds. However, if schools on a widespread scale are to address disparities in student outcomes, it is necessary to work with the teachers who are already there. The importance of doing so is supported by Hattie's (2009) comprehensive meta-analysis that highlights that the predominant influence on student achievement is the teacher.

The literature suggests that professional development that is most likely to have an impact on teaching is sustained over time, focuses on specific instructional strategies or content areas, involves teachers collectively rather than individually, is coherent, and uses active learning (Garet et al., 2001; Snow-Runner & Lauer, 2005). Peer coaching in the classroom is emerging as an important facet of teacher professional development that is linked with improved student learning (Joyce & Showers, 2002; Neufield & Roper, 2003). Yet, as is highlighted in Chapter 4, surprisingly little research directly links professional development with student learning. Yoon et al. (2007) reviewed more than 1,300 studies that purport to address the impact of teacher professional development on student learning, finding only 9 of the studies to meet rigorous criteria of evidence. The 9 studies found that student achievement increased by an average effect size of .54, or put another way, an improvement index of 21 percentile points, as a result of teachers' professional development, which Yoon and colleagues described as a "moderate effect" (p. 2). Clearly, there is a compelling need for well-designed, larger scale research on the impact of teacher professional development on student achievement.

Overall, research on teacher professional development for culturally responsive pedagogy is thin, examining impact on teachers, but not on students. None of the studies Yoon et al. (2007) reviewed focused on culturally responsive pedagogy. Most case studies that have been done explore the impact of specific kinds of professional development programs, such as a series of workshops (DeJaeghere & Zhang, 2008), inquiry-based graduate courses (Jennings & Smith, 2002; Sleeter, 2009), teacher networks (El-Haj, 2003), teacher collaborative inquiry groups (Hynds, 2007), community-based learning (Fickel, 2005; Moll & González, 1994), and sustained workshops combined with classroom-based coaching (Zozakiewicz & Rodriguez, 2007). But there has been no systematic research program into how teacher professional development on culturally responsive pedagogy changes teacher practice, let alone impacts on students.

I will suggest how one conceptualizes the nature and basis of disparities is important in the design of professional development for culturally relevant pedagogy. One can distinguish between two quite different designs: technical-rational designs in which experts teach pedagogical practices to teachers, and designs that attempt to reposition teachers as learners in relationship to their students and students' communities.

Technical-rational models of professional development

Technical-rational models have long dominated education (Mehan, Hubbard, & Datnow, 2010). Sleeter and Montecinos (1999) explain that under a technical-rational model, "teaching entails a series of technical decisions made by experts who have a claim to authority. This claim rests on two premises: ownership of a domain of a morally neutral set of facts and the belief that those facts represent law-like generalizations that can be applied to particular cases" (p. 116). It follows then that professional development based on a technical-rational approach assumes that underachievement of minoritized students can be addressed by experts teaching teachers specific skills and understandings to use in the classroom. Two examples illustrate, both of which were structured in accordance with research on effective professional development.

Haviland and Rodriguez-Kiino (2008) reported the results of a program designed to shift White professors' deficit thinking about Latino students in a small college in the western part of the U.S. They explain that the course was based on the assumption that professors would shift their practices if they were more aware of the problem and knew more about culturally responsive pedagogy. The program entailed a 6-week online course teaching about Latino culture and culturally responsive teaching, and a 3-day summer institute where professors could share ideas and work together. Pre- and post-interviews, structured classroom observations, and student surveys revealed mixed results across the faculty. While some professors reported large gains in awareness, others found the program irrelevant to their practice.

Zozakiewicz and Rodriguez (2007) studied the impact of professional development for elementary and middle school teachers in California, towards making science gender-inclusive, inquiry-based, and multicultural. This program included a summer institute, classroom visits, a workshop focused on teacher-identified needs, and meetings to discuss progress. The summer institute taught theoretical underpinnings for sociocultural transformative teaching, and classroom practices that connect science with learning. Interview, focus group, and survey data revealed high satisfaction with the program and self-reported improvements in teaching for most teachers. However, Zozakiewicz and Rodriguez found that some of the teachers focused more on science aspects of the professional development rather than issues of culture and equity.

In both of these cases, while there was some self-reported shift in understandings and practices, there was also a significant amount of resistance that took the form of teachers viewing culture as irrelevant. While improving teaching of minoritized students may well require teachers to learn new knowledge and skills, unlearning deficit theorizing also requires that teachers reframe their construction of students. Timperley et al. (2007) reviewed 8 empirical studies of professional development programs designed to reframe teachers' constructions of students. The focus of the various programs differed, ranging from gender positioning, to disability positioning, to expectations for achievement of low-income students. The authors identified characteristics common to the programs, such as infrastructural supports, teacher engagement in the learning process, and use of external expertise. What strikes me, however, is that most of the programs used a technical-rational approach to teacher learning in the sense that "experts" taught knowledge and skills to teachers that teachers could then use with minoritized students. Implicitly, the programs replicated power imbalances in the wider society in which minoritized students themselves have little or no voice. Teachers occupy the position of "expert" in relationship to the students, just as professional developers occupy the position of "expert" in relationship to the teachers.

Professional development that repositions teacher-student relationships

A co-construction model of teacher professional development that repositions teachers as learners, and minoritized students as teachers, would seek to reconstruct this power imbalance, placing students as the 'experts' who know best what works for them. In that way, this model fits with emancipatory approaches to addressing disparities. But, as Cook-Sather (2006) argues, repositioning students as active agents in the reform of schooling is both profoundly democratic and profoundly difficult, "Because schools are set up on premises of prediction, control, and management, anything that challenges those premises is hard to accomplish within formal educational contexts" (p. 381). She argues that convincing educators not only to listen to students, but to develop an ongoing process of engaging with what students say, even when what they say destabilizes core assumptions teachers hold, contradicts deeply held norms about teaching. Yet, one might truly regard students as the "experts" about teaching and learning since they are the beneficiaries of what happens in school every day.

Several published studies have examined what students have to say about school, with the intention that student voice should inform school reform and teacher learning. In the U.S., these include Poplin and Weere's (1992) study in Southern California, Wilson and Corbett's (2001) extensive body of interviews with students in Philadelphia, and Storz's (2008) study of more than 200 students in four Midwestern urban schools. There has been a small amount of research on teachers' learning through listening to their students. Martin and Hand (2009) report a case study of a science teacher in the U.S. learning to shift from teacher-centered to student-centered teaching; as student voice increased in the teacher's classroom, the researchers found that students' ownership over their learning and the quality of students' argumentation also increased. In New Zealand, Baskerville (2011) reported a process of using storytelling in the classroom to activate student voice and build cross-cultural understandings and relationships; as the two teachers took part in the storytelling alongside the students, everyone in the classroom was positioned as both teacher and learner.

There has been some investigation into engaging preservice teachers with student voice as a way of prompting them to rethink their assumptions about students. Cook-Sather (2010) in the U.S. has developed a well-conceptualized process in which high school students act as consultants to preservice teachers about teaching and learning. Her process intentionally disrupts the traditional positioning of the teacher as the source of knowledge and students as passive receivers of knowledge, and works to build a reciprocal relationship in which teachers and students can talk with each other about classroom teaching and learning.

But missing is research that links teacher professional development in culturally responsive pedagogy with an impact on not just the teacher, but also the teacher's students. Documenting that link, especially through a program designed around repositioning, is the focus of this book.

Overview of This Book

Drawing on a range of evaluation data of one program implemented over a period of several years in 49 secondary schools, this book addresses the following question: To what extent can schools improve outcomes for minoritized students through relationship-based professional development in culturally responsive pedagogy? The book is based on a large-scale evaluation of a theory-driven school reform project called Te Kotahitanga, which focuses on improving the educational achievement of Māori students in public secondary schools in New Zealand.

In Chapter 2, Russell Bishop orients readers to the historical and conceptual basis of Te Kotahitanga, developed and implemented by him and Mere Berryman at the University of Waikato in New Zealand. After situating the project within work for self-determination among Māori people, he describes the research that initiated this project, which focused on analyzing how different stakeholders—teachers, administrators, parents, and students—understood the underachievement of Māori students. It was from these narratives that the Effective Teaching Profile, which guides the project's professional development program, was developed. In Chapter 3, Mere Berryman explains the theoretical basis and cycle of activities of the Te Kotahitanga professional development program. She introduces readers to the in-school facilitators, explains how they are prepared, and how they work with teachers in their schools using a relationship-based process to help the teachers learn to use relationship-based culturally responsive pedagogy in their own classrooms.

In Chapter 4, Luanna Meyer discusses the large-scale evaluation that provides data reported in the rest of the book. A team from Victoria University of Wellington, New Zealand conducted a three-year, Ministry of Education–funded, external evaluation of the project in 22 of the 33 schools implementing the professional development initiative at the time of the evaluation. Some of these schools had participated in the project for more than 4 years while others were completing their second year of participation. After setting out considerations for evaluating teacher professional development, she describes the evidence-based framework that was used for this evaluation, including the research design, data sources, and process of data analysis.

Chapters 5, 6, and 7 then share what was learned about the impact of this professional development program. In Chapter 5, Anne Hynds and Christine Sleeter examine how teachers and facilitators perceived and experienced the professional development program. Enthusiasm for it was very high; findings detail how partnerships were built within the school to support Māori student learning, as well as challenges teachers and facilitators faced in the process of restructuring pedagogy. In Chapter 6, Catherine Savage and Rawiri Hindle examine changes that the evaluation team observed in classrooms, and how teachers described and understood changes in their own pedagogy. Based on 330 systematic classroom observations in 22 project schools, 98 comparison observations in 10 non-project schools, and interviews with more than 165 teaching staff, this chapter shows how and to what extent the Te Kotahitanga professional development program changed teacher practice. In Chapter 7, Wally Penetito, Rawiri Hindle, Anne Hynds, Catherine Savage, and Larissa Kus report data examining the extent to which these classroom changes actually made an impact on Māori students. Using achievement and retention data, interview data with students, and interview data with families of students, the chapter details positive ways in which students were affected, as well as some limitations of the program's impact and challenges in attempting to gauge the impact of a professional development program given the complexity of factors that affect student outcomes in schools.

Finally, in the concluding chapter, Russell Bishop, Christine Sleeter, and Luanna Meyer reflect on what can be learned from the evaluation of this professional development initiative for culturally responsive pedagogy. The chapter first reflects on what the University of Waikato team learned from the evaluation and how it has made use of those insights. The chapter then reflects on the power of a relationship-based approach to teaching and learning that is grounded in student voice, as well as inherent limitations of such as approach for taking on the wider system of colonization and racism that affects minoritized student learning. The chapter concludes with some reflection on how this project might speak to audiences internationally, including potentials as well as limitations of exporting a project that is initiated in response to a crisis facing a minoritized group in a particular national context.

The book shows the extent to which a well-conceptualized and culturally grounded, theory-based program in culturally responsive pedagogy, supported by a well-conceptualized professional development program, can shift teacher practices and understandings. These shifts can lead to a reduction in educational disparities of minoritized students, as well as support for the students as culturally located human beings. While this project addresses Māori students' educational achievement as a means of addressing educational disparities, it is clear that the messages drawn from this study are applicable beyond the shores of New Zealand, because the educational experiences of Māori people are common to many Indigenous and other minoritized peoples in countries around the world. In this way, this detailed, in-depth analysis will resonate with those interested in addressing what was identified earlier as being a major issue facing Western countries currently, the seemingly immutable educational disparities between children for whom the education systems were designed and for those whom have been minoritized by these systems.

· 2 ·

TE KOTAHITANGA: KAUPAPA MĀORI IN MAINSTREAM CLASSROOMS

Russell Bishop, University of Waikato

This then is the great humanistic and historical task of the oppressed: to liberate themselves and their oppressors as well. The oppressors, who oppress, exploit and rape by virtue of their power, cannot find in this power the strength to liberate either the oppressed or themselves. Only power that springs from the weakness of the oppressed will be sufficiently strong to free both.

Paolo Freire, *Pedagogy of the Oppressed* (1972, p. 21)

The Te Kotahitanga project aims to address education disparities between European New Zealand students and Māori students in secondary schools, primarily by shifting pedagogy in the classroom. This chapter sets out to present the genesis, theoretical foundations, research base, and pedagogical implications of the project. The first section orients readers to Kaupapa Māori, which is the theoretical frame that guided the development of Te Kotahitanga. The second section examines what a culturally responsive pedagogy of relations that arises from Kaupapa Māori theory might look like in mainstream schools, and how Te Kotahitanga operationalized Kaupapa Māori research in developing its vision for pedagogical reform. Finally, the last section of the chapter reflects on the power of narratives from within marginalized communities for charting the pathway for reform.

Kaupapa Māori as Theory

Kaupapa Māori is a discourse of proactive theory and practice that emerged from within the wider revitalization of Māori communities that developed in New Zealand following the rapid Māori urbanization in the 1950's and 1960's. This movement grew further in the 1970's and by the late 1980's had developed as a political consciousness among Māori people, promoting the revitalization of Māori cultural aspirations, preferences and practices as a philosophical and productive educational stance and resistance to the hegemony of the dominant discourse. As Smith (1997) explains:

> Māori communities armed with the new critical understandings of the shortcomings of the state and structural analyses began to assert transformative actions to deal with the twin crises of language demise and educational underachievement for themselves. (p. 171)

Smith (1997) goes on to explain that especially since the advent of Te Kohanga Reo (language nests: Māori medium pre-schools) in 1982, Kaupapa Māori has become "an influential and coherent philosophy and practice for Māori conscientisation, resistance and transformative praxis to advance Māori cultural capital and learning outcomes within education and schooling" (p. 423). The Kaupapa Māori approach developed among Māori groups across a wide range of educational sectors, such as Te Kohanga Reo, Kura Kaupapa Māori (Māori medium schools), Wharekura (Māori medium secondary schools) and Waananga Māori (Māori tertiary institutions), and also included other groups such as the New Zealand Māori Council, The Māori Congress, Māori Health and Welfare bodies, Iwi (tribal) Authorities and, most recently, a Māori political party. For Māori, the specific intention was to achieve "increased autonomy over their own lives and cultural welfare" (Smith, 1992, p. 12). In education, this call for autonomy grew in response to the lack of programs and processes within existing educational institutions that were designed to "reinforce, support or proactively co-opt Māori cultural aspirations in ways which are desired by Māori themselves" (Smith, 1992, p. 12). Smith further suggests that the wish for autonomy also challenged the "increasing abdication by the State of its 1840 contractual obligation [The Treaty of Waitangi] to protect Māori cultural interests" (p. 10). In other words, if the government, granted the right to govern in Article 1 of the Treaty of Waitangi[1] (Durie, 1998), was unable or unwilling to facilitate Māori protection of cultural treasures that were guaranteed in Article 2 of the Treaty, then Māori groups would need to take on this task themselves.

This call for autonomy is operationalized in a Kaupapa Māori approach as self-determination (tino rangatiratanga) by and for Māori people (Bishop, 1996; Durie, 1995, 1998; Pihama, Cram, & Walker, 2002; G. Smith, 1997; L. Smith, 1999), which means the right to determine one's own destiny, to define what that destiny will be, and to define and pursue means of attaining that destiny. However, there is a clear understanding among Māori people that such autonomy is relative, not absolute, that it is self-determination in *relation to others*. As such, Māori calls for self-determination are often misunderstood by non-Māori people. It is not a call for separatism or non-interference, nor is it a call for non-Māori people to stand back and leave Māori alone, in effect to relinquish all responsibility for the ongoing relationship between the peoples of New Zealand. Rather it is a call for all those involved in education in New Zealand to reposition themselves in relation to these emerging aspirations of Māori people for an autonomous voice (Bishop, 1994; Smith, 1997; Durie, 1998). In other words, Kaupapa Māori seeks to operationalize Māori people's aspirations to restructure power relationships to the point where partners can be autonomous and interact from this position rather than from one of subordination or dominance.

The indigenous position on self-determination, therefore, in practice means that individuals should be free to determine their own goals and make sense of the world in their own culturally generated manner. However, as Young (2004) emphasizes, self-determining individuals cannot ignore their interdependence with others and the claims that others may have to their own self-determination. Therefore, the implications for educational institutions are that participants in these institutions should structure and conduct them in such a way as to seek to mediate these potential tensions by actively minimizing domination, coordinating actions, resolving conflicts and negotiating relationships.

Māori attempts to promote this indigenous peoples' understanding of self-determination has to date been developed primarily in separate Māori medium institutions such as Te Kohanga Reo and Kura Kaupapa Māori. However, these efforts have messages for the mainstream (where most Māori children are enrolled), for as Smith (1992, 1997) has suggested, these projects share some common elements that have formed out of the cycle of conscientization, resistance and transformative praxis that typifies the struggle of Māori people that, although these elements arise from the Māori education sector, and Kura Kaupapa Māori in particular, they may also speak to the "general crisis in schooling" for Māori (pp. 18 and 446).

This chapter sets out to examine what might constitute Māori experiences of successful Māori innovations in education "speaking to" the wider crisis in Māori education, in particular disparities in achievement in mainstream educational settings. This examination is further informed by a range of studies into effective innovation in Māori medium schooling (Alton-Lee, 2003; Bishop et al., 2001; Smith, 1997), and focuses upon, in particular, Māori metaphor that might provide solutions to the Māori educational crisis in mainstream settings. The metaphors used are those that Smith (1997) identifies are fundamental to Māori medium schooling and are here expanded to provide a picture of what might constitute an appropriate pedagogy for Māori students in mainstream schools.

- **Rangatiratanga (relative autonomy/self-determination):** Fundamental to Māori educational institutions is the concept of rangatiratanga, which literally means chiefly control. However, increasingly it has taken on its figurative meaning of self-determination which, as is described above, means the right to determine one's own destiny, to define what that destiny will be and to define and pursue a means of attaining that destiny, in relation to others, this notion of relations being fundamental to Māori epistemologies.
- **Taonga Tuku Iho (cultural aspirations):** Literally meaning the treasures from the ancestors, this phrase nowadays is almost always used in its metaphoric sense as meaning the cultural aspirations that Māori people hold for their children and include those messages that guide our relationships and interaction patterns such as manaakitanga (caring), kaitiakitanga (oversight), and mana motuhake (respect for specialness). Above all this message means that Māori language, knowledge, culture and values are normal, valid and legitimate, and indeed are valid guides to classroom interactions. The implications of this principle for educational contexts is that educators need to create contexts where to be Māori is to be normal, where Māori cultural identities are valued, valid and legitimate—in other words where Māori children can be themselves.
- **Ako (reciprocal learning):** Literally meaning to teach and to learn, this term metaphorically emphasizes reciprocal learning, which means

that the teacher does not have to be the fountain of all knowledge, but rather should be able to create contexts for learning where the students can enter the learning conversation.

- **Kia piki ake i nga raruraru o te kainga (mediation of socio-economic and home difficulties):** Participation in Kura Kaupapa Māori reaches into Māori homes and brings parents and families into the activities of the school because it is understood that where parents are incorporated into the education of their children on terms they can understand and approve of, then children do better at school.

- **Whānau (extended family):** Whānau means an extended family. Used in a metaphoric sense, educational whānau attempt to develop relationships, organizations and operational practices based on similar principles to those which order a traditional whānau.

- **Kaupapa (collective vision, philosophy):** Just as Kura Kaupapa Māori have a collective vision, a kaupapa that provides guidelines for what constitutes excellence in Māori education that connects with "Māori aspirations, politically, socially, economically and spiritually" (Smith, 1992, p. 23). To do so, mainstream institutions need such a philosophy or agenda for achieving excellence in both languages and cultures that make up the world of Māori children.

Implications of these metaphors

This series of metaphors, drawn from the experiences of Kaupapa Māori educational theorizing and practice, and expanded here to address Māori students in mainstream settings, does provide us with a picture of the sort of alternative educational relations and interactions that are possible where educators draw upon an alternative culture than that previously dominant. This picture consists of a collective vision, focusing on the need to address Māori students' achievement, that identifies the need for power over reciprocal decision making to be constituted within relationships and interactions constructed as within a collective whānau context. Whānau relationships would enact reciprocal and collaborative pedagogies in order to promote educational relationships between students, between pupils and teachers (also, between whānau members in decision making about the school), and between the home and the school as a means of promoting excellence in education. One wider indicator of this pattern would be the development of inextricable two-way connections between the home and the school.

Such a pattern of metaphor also creates an image of classroom relations and interactions where students are able to participate on their own terms— terms that are determined by the student—because the very pedagogic process holds this as a central value. Further, the terms are to be culturally determined, through the incorporation and reference to the sense-making processes of the student. Learning is to be reciprocal and interactive, home and school learning is to be interrelated, learners are to be connected to each other and learn with and from each other. In addition, a common set of goals and principles guides the process. Further, just as using Māori metaphors for research repositions researchers within Māori sense-making contexts (Bishop, 1996, 2005), so too does using new metaphors for pedagogy reposition teachers within contexts where students' sense-making processes offer new opportunities for them to engage with learning. In these contexts, learners' experiences, representations of these experiences, and sense-making processes are legitimated.

In detail, therefore, such a pattern of metaphor suggests that educators can create learning contexts that will address the learning engagement and improve the achievement of Māori students by developing learning-teaching relationships where the following notions are paramount. That is,

- *where power is shared*: where learners can initiate interactions; learners' right to self-determination over learning styles, and sense-making processes are regarded as fundamental to power-sharing relationships; collaborative critical reflection is part of an ongoing critique of power relationships;
- *where culture counts*: where classrooms are places where learners can bring "who they are" to the learning interactions in complete safety, and their knowledges are 'acceptable' and 'legitimate';
- *where learning is interactive and dialogic*: learners are able to be co-inquirers, that is, raisers of questions and evaluators of questions and answers; learning is active, problem-based, integrated and holistic; learning positionings are reciprocal (ako) and knowledge is co-created; classrooms are places where young people's sense-making processes and knowledges are validated and developed in collaboration with others;
- *where connectedness is fundamental to relations*: teachers are committed to and inextricably connected to their students and the community

and vice versa; school and home/parental aspirations are comple-
mentary.

- *where there is a common vision*: a common agenda for what constitutes
  excellence for Māori in education.

Drawing on Gay (2010) and Villegas and Lucas (2002), who identify
the importance of a culturally responsive pedagogy, and Sidorkin (2002)
and Cummins (1996), who propose that relations ontologically precede all
other concerns in education, such a pattern might well be termed a Culturally
Responsive Pedagogy of Relations.

A Culturally Responsive Pedagogy of Relations

With this framework in mind, this chapter now seeks to examine what
a culturally responsive pedagogy of relations might look like in practice.
Te Kotahitanga: Improving the Educational Achievement of Māori students in Mainstream Schools (Bishop et al., 2003) is a large-scale Kaupapa
Māori research/professional development project that aims to improve the
educational achievement of Māori students. It does so through operationalizing Māori people's cultural aspirations for self-determination within non-
dominating relations of interdependence by developing classroom relations
and interactions and in-school institutionalized processes for this purpose.
Māori metaphors inform educational theorizing and practice in ways that seek
to mediate the ongoing educational crisis facing Māori people in mainstream
education from within a Kaupapa Māori framework.

The project commenced in 2001, seeking to address the self determination
of Māori secondary school students by talking with them and other participants
in their education about just what is involved in limiting and/or improving
their educational achievement. The project gathered a number of narratives
of students' classroom experiences and meanings by the process of collaborative storying (Bishop, 1996), from a range of engaged and non-engaged Māori
students (as defined by their schools), in five non-structurally modified mainstream secondary schools. These stories were complemented by those parenting these students, their principals, and their teachers.

Cook-Sather (2002) suggests that an approach that authorizes student
perspectives is essential to reform education because of the various ways that
it can improve educational practice, re-inform existing conversations about

educational reform, and point to the discussions and reform effects yet to be undertaken. From a detailed analysis of the literature she identified that such authorizing of students' experiences and understandings can directly improve educational practice in that when teachers listen to and learn from students, they can begin to see the world from the perspective of those students. This in turn can help teachers make what they teach more accessible to students. These actions can also contribute to the conceptualization of teaching, learning, and the ways we study as being more collaborative processes. Further, students can feel empowered when they are taken seriously and attended to as knowledgeable participants in learning conversations, and they can be motivated to participate constructively in their education. In addition, she further identifies that authorizing students' perspectives is a major way of addressing power imbalances in classrooms in order for students' voices to have legitimacy in the learning setting.

Such understandings inform this project for it is a Kaupapa Māori position that when teachers share their power with students, they will better understand the world of the 'others' and those 'othered' by power differentials, and students will be better able to participate and engage more successfully in educational systems on their own culturally constituted terms. In turn, teachers will create culturally appropriate and responsive contexts for learning (Bishop et al., 2003; Gay, 2010) through drawing upon a different pattern of metaphor such as described earlier in this chapter. In this way Māori students will be able to interact with teachers and others in ways that legitimate who they are and how they make sense of the world. It is suggested that such positive, inclusive interactions will lead to improved student engagement in learning. Numerous studies (Applebee, 1996; Bruner, 1996; Fisher et al., 1981; Widdowson, Dixon, & Moore, 1996) identify that improving student engagement is a necessary condition for improving educational achievement. Further, improved student on-task engagement has been identified as a moderate to good predictor of long-term student achievement (Fisher et al., 1981; Gage & Berliner, 1992; Widdowson et al., 1996; Yesseldyke & Christensen, 1998).

Fundamental to Kaupapa Māori theorizing is an analysis of that which might limit Māori advancement in education. Therefore, as part of this project, in addition to the students, those parenting the students, their principals (as the agenda setters of the schools), and a representation of their teachers (approximately 23% of the teachers in the 5 schools) were also asked to narrate their experiences in the education of Māori students. In this way, the students' experiences could be understood within the wider context of their education and their lives in general. The analysis of these narratives provided some very illuminating information about the positions taken by people in relation to one another, the consequent pattern of interdependence and the potential of a variety of discursive positionings for perpetuating or offering solutions to the problem of educational disparities.

The students

Whilst there were differences between the experiences of the engaged and non-engaged students, most students reported being Māori in a mainstream secondary school was for them a negative experience. Few reported that being Māori in their classrooms, currently or in the past, was a positive experience. Further, most of the students identified that the relationships with their teachers was the most influential factor in their ability to achieve in the classroom. In particular, the students emphasized that the ways in which teachers taught, that is how they interacted with Māori students, influenced them into either becoming engaged in their learning or not. To a lesser extent, students identified how issues related to their home experiences, and to structural issues within the school impacted on their learning and contributed to their educational experience being less productive. Overall, the majority of the students interviewed wanted to be able to attend school, to have positive educational experiences and to achieve. Most of all, however, they wanted to be able to do this as Māori.

In so doing they alerted us of the need for education to be responsive to them as culturally located people, and in this way to the emerging literature on the creation of learning contexts and how these contexts might be constituted as appropriate and responsive to the culturally generated sense-making processes of the students. This notion of cultural responsiveness (Gay, 2010; Nieto, 2000) offers a means whereby teachers can acknowledge and address Māori students' self-determination within their classrooms by creating learning contexts wherein the learning relationships and interactions are such that Māori students can bring themselves into what Grumet (1995) terms the "conversation that makes sense of the world" (p. 19).

Those parenting (Whānau)

Those parenting Māori students (their whānau) identified that the major influence on Māori students' educational achievement was the quality of their

children's relationship with their teachers. These whānau members acknowledged that they had to take some responsibility for ensuring their children did
well in the educational setting and that the relationship they had with their
children contributed to their success at school. However, there remained a
strong expectation that schools should take some responsibility for providing
their children with good experiences at school. If this was to be achieved,
according to the whānau members, the schools and the teachers needed to
have a greater understanding of things Māori, including the reality that Māori
people have their own cultural values, aspirations and ways of knowing. This
realization was seen as vital so as to allow the culture of the child to be present,
recognized and respected within the school and the classroom. This expectation was also raised by both student groups.

The principals

Like the students and those parenting, the principals also drew primarily upon
the discourse of relationships to identify the main influences on Māori students'
educational achievement. In particular, the principals identified that the attitude of the teacher was crucial to the development of positive learning relationships between the teacher and their Māori students. Teachers' low expectations
of Māori students and the need for teachers to adjust to the individual learning
requirements of their students were also identified as critical factors.

The principals identified that one way teachers might facilitate a more
responsive relationship was by recognizing Māori students' culture and taking cognizance of Māori cultural aspirations and notions of belonging. They
identified that developing more culturally responsive relationships required
schools to build Māori pedagogies that went beyond the limited inclusion of
Māori cultural iconography into their curriculum and programs. Principals saw
this type of initiative as a means of enhancing the relationships between Māori
students and staff, and as a means of gaining positive support from parents of
Māori students. Pivotal to this was the building and maintaining of relationships with their Māori communities.

The teachers

Contrary to the narratives of experience provided by the students, those parenting and the principals, most teachers identified factors from within the
discourse of the child and their home as having the greatest influence on

Māori students' educational achievement. In particular, teachers perceived deficits within the home, or problems that Māori students brought with them to school from home as having the major influence on Māori students' educational achievement.

In terms of influences outside of the school, teachers identified problems of home background and socio-economic problems, leading to greater mobility and transience of Māori students, as being problematic. Deficit influences were further elaborated by teachers' perceptions of Māori students' lack of access to resources, inadequate nutrition, condoned absenteeism, access to drugs, alcohol and other anti-social behaviors in the community, participation in work outside of school, and inadequate parental support or positive role models.

In addition, teachers identified the problems that Māori students cause when they are at school. Teachers argued that Māori student underachievement was the result of the low-level aspirations of Māori students and their lack of motivation and poor behavior. Teachers also spoke of the negative influence of peers (Māori), and the wasted talent of Māori students being unwilling to stand out from the crowd (a perceived cultural issue). Teachers identified that Māori students were disorganized, not prepared for their classes or for learning, and difficult to discipline. Many teachers expressed a great deal of disillusionment about their ability to effect change in the face of these constant pressures.

Although teachers as a group were less convinced that in-class relationships were of importance to Māori students' educational achievement, a small group of teachers did identify that positive relationships were built in their classrooms through their respecting the cultural knowledge and aspirations of Māori students. They further suggested that these actions resulted in improved student behavior, engagement and involvement in learning.

The teachers identified that structural and systemic issues had the least influence on Māori students' educational achievement. These included curriculum demands being placed upon teachers and high student and staff turnover. Overall, however, the teachers argued strongly about the perceived deficits of the child/home as having the most significant impact on Māori students' educational achievement.

Interpretation of the narratives of experience: Development of the analytical model

A critical reading of the narratives of experience identified three main discourses within which the participant groups positioned themselves when identifying and explaining both positive and negative influences on Māori students' educational achievement. There was the discourse of the child and home, which included those influences that were to be found outside of the school and the classroom. There was the discourse of structure and systems or those influences outside of the classroom, but pertaining to the school itself and/or the wider education system. There was the discourse of relationships and classroom interaction patterns, which included all those influences that were identified as being within the classroom.

This schema was used in the analysis of all the narratives as a means of comparing the relative weightings that the various groups of interview participants gave to each set of influences within the major discourses, or which discourse each group drew upon most frequently. This was undertaken by compiling frequency tables of unit ideas (see Bishop et al., 2003). The narratives were coded according to idea units, and the number of times those units were repeated across the schools, rather than within each school. In this way we were attempting to develop a picture from across all the schools, as opposed to letting the experiences of one school, or even one articulate student or teacher, dominate. Therefore the frequency count, as shown in Figure 2.1, is a

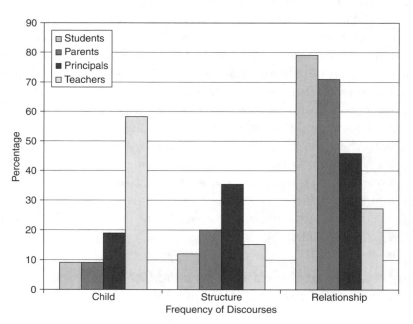

Figure 2.1 Frequency of Discourses
Bishop et al. (2003)

tally of idea units. These idea units were then listed according to the discourse they illustrated and ranked according to the number of times such idea units were mentioned in the narratives.

This analysis of the narratives was conducted within the same Kaupapa Māori approach that had been used in the process of interviewing. Primacy in the interviewing approach was given to acknowledging the self-determination of the interview participants to be able to explain their own experiences in their own culturally constituted terms. The interviews were undertaken as in-depth, semi-structured conversations (Bishop & Glynn, 1999) and sought to minimize the imposition of the researchers' own sense making and theorizing on the experiences and explanations of the interview participants. As a result, in the construction of the narratives, emphasis was given to the meanings that interview participants had ascribed to their experiences and in this way produced a representation that the participants would legitimate.

Similarly, the research team were particular to ensure that coding the narratives was based on what the experiences meant to the speaker rather than what it meant to us as researchers. For example, some of the students' references to peer influences may be coded to relationships, whereas for parents and teachers these idea units may be coded as part of the discourse of the child and home. All of those who were coding were fully conversant with the process of constructing narratives of experience through the process of spiral discourse/collaborative storying (Bishop, 1996) and, therefore, read the narratives widely so as to identify the meaning that the interview participants had attributed to that particular issue. In addition, for purposes of consistency, the coding was undertaken by a small number of the research team who were both familiar with the process of collaborative storying and who had developed a common agreement as to what constituted idea units, themes, sub-themes and, more important, how participants positioned themselves in relation to the various discourses.

The interpretative process, drawing on both qualitative and quantitative means of measurement, provided frequency bars for all four interviewee groups. When viewed together as in Figure 2.1, they provide a clear picture of the conflict in theorizing that is to be found about the lived experiences of Māori students, a picture that, from anecdotal evidence, is to be found time and again in New Zealand schools. In addition, while it may be tempting to attribute significance to some minor differences in numbers or percentages, it is the overall pattern of differences that is of importance to this argument.

As this analysis came from interviews in only a small number of schools, it is suggested that rather than representing firm generalizations, Figure 2.1

provides a means of ascribing a rough weighting to each discourse that might indicate patterns and trends that one may well find in other, similar settings. Therefore the picture presented here is one that others can reflect upon to critically evaluate where they position themselves when constructing their own images, principles and practices in relation to Māori or other minoritized students within their own settings. Indeed, when we share these stories with teachers in professional development and other workshops, many people voice their own familiarity with these experiences and also express that reading these narratives of experience enables them to reflect upon their own discursive positioning and its potential impact upon their students' learning. We present these stories, not so others can generalize, but rather so that educators can particularize as to their own experiences.

Discursive positioning

It is clear from the pattern shown in Figure 2.1 that the main influences on Māori students' educational achievement that people identify varies according to where they position themselves within the three discourses. Those who identify that, from their experiences, in-class relationships between teachers and students (and others involved in the educational community) have the greatest influence on Māori students' educational achievement stand in contrast to those who identify the main influences as being Māori students themselves, their homes and/or the structure of the schools—that is, influences from outside of the classroom. What is problematic for education is that it is mainly teachers who position themselves in significant numbers within this latter group. In so doing, a large proportion of the teachers were pathologizing Māori students' lived experiences by explaining their lack of educational achievement in deficit terms, either as being within the child or their home, or within the structure of the school.

Positioning within this latter group also means that the speakers tended to blame someone or something else outside of their area of influence, and as a result, they suggest that they can have very little responsibility for the outcomes of these influences. The main consequence of such deficit theorizing for the quality of teachers' relationships with Māori students and for classroom interactions is that teachers tend to have low expectations of Māori students' ability or a fatalistic attitude in the face of systemic imponderables. This in turn creates a downward spiraling, self-fulfilling prophecy of Māori student achievement and failure.

Further, those who position themselves here see very few solutions to the problems. In terms of agency then, this is a very non-agentic position in that there is not much an individual can do from this position other than change the child's family situation or the education 'system', solutions often well outside of their own agency. Therefore, along with others (Gay, 2010; Kincheloe & Steinberg, 1997; Nieto, 2000; Wagstaff & Fusarelli, 1995), it is suggested that teachers' deficit theorizing is the major impediment to Māori students' educational achievement. As Bruner (1996) identifies, unless these positionings—these theorizings by teachers—are addressed and overcome, teachers will not be able to realize their agency and little substantial change will occur.

Indeed, Shields, Bishop and Mazawi (2005), in three case studies of the impact of pathologizing theories and practices on Navaho, Māori and Bedouin peoples, found that pathologizing the lived experiences of these three peoples was all pervasive and was deeply rooted in psychological, epistemological, social and historical discourses. They found that,

> pathologizing is manifested in education and schooling in knowledge, power, agency, structures and relationships including both the pedagogical and home-schooling relationships. In fact pathologizing in the form of deficit theorizing is the major impediment to the achievement of minoritized students; an understanding that is only too well known by indigenous peoples such as Māori and which forms the basis of Māori resistance to such theorizing. (p. 196)

In contrast, speakers who position themselves within the discourse of relationships and interactions understand that within this space, explanations that seek to address the power imbalances between the various participants in the relationships can be developed and implemented. In addition, these speakers tend to accept responsibility for their part in the relationships and are clear that they have agency, in that they are active participants in educational relationships. That is, speakers who position themselves here have a personal understanding that they can bring about change and indeed are responsible for bringing about changes in the educational achievement of Māori students.

Uses of the narratives

The narratives of experience, which appear in *Culture Speaks* (Bishop & Berryman, 2006), and the collaborative storying approach, were therefore useful in a variety of ways in the project. First, the analysis of the narratives identifies the usefulness of the concept of discourse as a means of identifying the thoughts, words and actions shaped by power relations—those complex networks of images and metaphors that the various people in the stories drew upon to create meaning for themselves about their experiences with the education of Māori students. A critical reading of the narratives illustrates the impact of discursive positioning where some discourses offer solutions, others merely perpetuate the status quo. For example, despite most teachers wishing to make a difference for Māori students' educational achievement, they are not able to do so because of their discursive positioning, whereas others, discursively positioned differently, were able to offer numerous solutions to seemingly immutable changes. However, despite discursive positionings making available to teachers different concepts, metaphors, images and language that "derive from our occupation of subject positions within discourses" (Burr, 1995, p. 146), nonetheless, it is possible for teachers to positively and vehemently reject deficit theorizing as a means of explaining Māori students' educational achievement levels through discursive (re)positioning. It is not just a matter of our being subject to, or a product of, discourse; we have agency that allows us to (re)story our lives. As Burr (1995) argues, this narrative notion "allows us the possibility of personal and social change through our capacity to identify, understand and resist the discourse we are also subject to" (p. 153).

Second, the interviews for the narratives were conducted in a Kaupapa Māori manner (Bishop, 1997, 2005) in order that the participants were able to explain the meanings they constructed about their educational experiences either as or with Māori students in ways that acknowledged their self-determination. The students, for example, clearly identified the main influences on their educational achievement by articulating the impact and consequences of their living in a marginalized space. That is, they explained how they were perceived in pathological terms by their teachers and how this has had a negative effect up on their lives. The whānau members and the principals were also able to identify the main influences upon Māori students' education from their own experiences. Similarly their teachers were able to explain the vast range of experiences and meanings they ascribed to these experiences so that they were able to speak in ways that legitimated their representations.

Third, the detailed narratives of experience (Bishop & Berryman, 2006) are used at the commencement of the professional development part of this project in response to Bruner's (1996) understanding that ". . . our interactions with others are deeply affected by our everyday intuitive theorizing about how other minds work" (p. 45). In other words, it is necessary to acknowledge that teachers are not simply vessels to be 'filled' by the expert outsider and that they do have strongly held theories of practice that affect and direct their practice and maybe some of these positions offer hope and maybe some don't. Indeed, it is clear from Figure 2.1 that many of these theories that teachers hold could well do with being challenged through the creation of a situation of cognitive, cultural and/or emotional dissonance by the provision of evidence that is outside of the usual experiences of the teachers, this evidence being used to critically reflect upon one's discursive positioning and the implications of this positioning for student outcomes. However, in line with the principles outlined in the earlier part of this chapter, it is clear that this challenging needs to be undertaken in a non-confrontational manner, one that acknowledges the mana (power) of the teachers where manaakitanga (caring for others) overrides aspirations to argue with, to chastise or to correct the ideas of one's guests. Therefore, as described in greater detail in Chapter 3, the focus of the professional development is to create a culturally appropriate and responsive context for learning wherein teachers can reflect upon the evidence of the experiences of others in similar circumstances, including, perhaps for the first time, the students. In this manner, teachers can critically evaluate where they position themselves when constructing their own images, principles and practices in relation to Māori students in their own classrooms. Sharing these vicarious experiences of schooling enables teachers to reflect upon their own understandings of Māori children's experiences, and consequently, upon their own theorizing/explanations about these experiences and their consequent practice. And in this way, teachers are afforded the opportunity to critically reflect upon their own discursive positioning and the implication of this positioning for their own agency and for Māori students' learning.

Fourth, the students were clear about how teachers, in changing how they related to and interacted with Māori students in their classrooms, could create a context for learning wherein Māori students' educational achievement could improve, again by placing the self-determination of Māori students at the center of classroom relationships and interactions. In addition, those others who positioned themselves within the relationship discourse were able to add numerous practical solutions to the problems of educational disparities facing Māori students. These stood in contrast to the very limited and mainly impractical (especially for classroom teachers) solutions offered by those who discursively positioned themselves within the other two discourses, that of the child and the home, and that of the social structure. It was from the ideas

Effective teachers of Māori students create a culturally appropriate and responsive context for learning in their classroom. In doing so they demonstrate the following understandings:

(1) They positively and vehemently reject deficit theorising as a means of explaining Māori students' educational achievement levels (and professional development projects need to ensure that this happens): and

(2) Teachers know and understand how to bring about change in Māori students' educational achievement and are professionally committed to doing so (and professional development projects need to ensure that this happens);

In the following observable ways:

(1) Manaakitanga: They care for the students as culturally located human beings above all else. (*Mana refers to authority and āaki, the task of urging someone to act. It refers to the task of building and nurturing a supportive and loving environment*).

(2) Mana motuhake: They care for the performance of their students. (*In modern times mana has taken on various meanings such as legitimation and authority and can also relate to an individual's or a group's ability to participate at the local and global level. Mana motuhake involves the development of personal or group identity and independence*).

(3) Whakapiringatanga: They are able to create a secure, well-managed learning environment by incorporating routine pedagogical knowledge with pedagogical imagination. (*Ngā tūranga takitahi me ngā mana whakahaere: involves specific individual roles and responsibilities that are required in order to achieve individual and group outcomes*).

(4) Wānanga: They are able to engage in effective teaching interactions with Māori students as Māori. (*As well as being known as Māori centres of learning wānanga as a learning forum involves a rich and dynamic sharing of knowledge. With this exchange of views ideas are given life and spirit through dialogue, debate and careful consideration in order to reshape and accommodate new knowledge*).

(5) Ako: They can use strategies that promote effective teaching interactions and relationships with their learners. (*Ako means to learn as well as to teach. It is both the acquisition of knowledge and the processing and imparting of knowledge. More importantly ako is a teaching-learning practice that is culturally specific and appropriate to Māori pedagogy*).

(6) Kotahitanga: They promote, monitor and reflect on outcomes that in turn lead to improvements in educational achievement for Māori students. (*Kotahitanga is a collaborative response towards a commonly held vision, goal or other such purpose or outcome*).

Figure 2.2 The Te Kotahitanga Effective Teaching Profile
Bishop et al. (2003)

of those who were positioned with the agentic relationships discourse that an Effective Teaching Profile was developed (see Figure 2.2).

This Effective Teaching Profile represents an operationalization of Māori peoples' aspirations for education as identified earlier this chapter and attempts to illustrate just what a Culturally Responsive Pedagogy of Relations in mainstream schools might look like in practice. Fundamental to this profile is the creation of a culturally responsive context for learning where teachers understand the need to explicitly reject deficit theorizing as a means of explaining Māori students' educational achievement levels, and where they take an agentic position in their theorizing about their practice. That is, they take a position where they see themselves as being able to express their professional commitment and responsibility to bringing about change in Māori students' educational achievement and accept professional responsibility for the learning of their students. This notion of agentic positioning addresses what Covey (2004) terms response ability, that is, teachers understanding the power they have to respond to who the students are and to what they bring to the classroom, often the invisible elements of culture; in short, the realization that learning comes about through changing the pedagogical relations and interactions in classrooms, not just changing one of the parties involved, be they the students or the teachers. These two central understandings are observable in these teachers' classrooms on a daily basis and are here again expressed and understood in terms of Māori metaphor: Manaakitanga, Mana Motuhake, Whakapiringatanga, Wananga, Ako and Kotahitanga, as reflected in Figure 2.2. In practice these mean that teachers: care for and acknowledge the mana of the students as culturally located individuals; have high expectations of the learning for students; are able to manage their classrooms so as to promote learning (which includes subject expertise); reduce their reliance upon transmission modes of education so as to engage in a range of discursive learning interactions with students or enable students to engage with others in these ways; know a range of strategies that can facilitate learning interactively; promote, monitor and reflect on learning outcomes that in turn lead to improvements in Māori student achievement and sharing this knowledge with the students so that they are let into the secret of what constitutes learning.

This profile, constructed from Māori students' suggestions (and reinforced by significant others involved in their education) as to how to improve education for themselves and their peers, matches the principles identified as metaphor earlier in this chapter. At center stage is the necessity for a common kaupapa or philosophy that rejects deficit thinking and pathologizing practices as a means of explaining Māori students' educational achievement. In concert is the underlying aspiration for rangatiratanga that promotes the agency of teachers to voice their professional commitment, willingness to engage in whānau relations, and interactions and reciprocal practices that are fundamental to addressing and promoting educational achievement for Māori students. The ways suggested for attaining success draw on Māori cultural aspirations in the way that the interview participants identified the need for caring as manaakitanga, for teachers demonstrating their high expectations and the creation of secure, well-managed learning settings, again in terms of the mana (power) of the students. The preferred discursive teaching interactions, strategies and the focus on formative assessment processes that are identified in the narratives also resonates with Māori cultural aspirations, above all, the creation of whānau type relations and interactions within classrooms and among teachers, students and their homes. Reciprocal approaches to learning, through cooperative learning strategies for example, in concert with the underlying aspiration for relative autonomy, underlies that desire to improve the educational achievement of Māori students in New Zealand through operationalising Māori people's cultural aspirations for self-determination within non-dominating relations of interdependence.

Conclusions

In this chapter an indigenous model of classroom relations and interactions is presented both theoretically and in practice. Methodologically, this model was developed from a theoretical examination of Māori people's resistance to neo-colonial hegemonies and also from their aspirations for and actualization of a pro-active, culturally constituted educational intervention in the educational crisis facing Māori people in Aotearoa/New Zealand today. This analysis took the form of an examination of what the metaphor fundamental to Kaupapa Māori generated educational institutions and Kaupapa Māori research might mean for mainstream educational institutions. These latter institutions, which attempt to provide an education for the vast majority of Māori students, are dominated by metaphors based in the dominant culture, such as hierarchical notions of self-determination, and are sites of struggle for Māori people, culture and language. The model suggests that mainstream classrooms that are constituted as places where power is shared between self-determining individuals within non-dominating relations of interdependence, where culture counts, learning is interactive, dialogic and spirals, participants are connected and committed to one another and where there is a common vision of excellence, will offer Māori students educational opportunities currently being denied to them.

Methodologically, putting this model into practice involved collaborative storying (Bishop, 1996, 2005) as a means of developing a series of narratives of experience. The resulting authorizing of student experiences and the meanings they constructed from these experiences address the power of determination over fundamental issues: who initiates research interactions, who determines what benefits there will be, who will benefit, whose reality or experiences (voice) are present in the narratives, with what authority do research participants speak, and to whom are researchers accountable (Bishop, 1996, 2005). The narratives were then used in the project in the following ways: (1) to identify a variety of discursive positions pertaining to Māori student achievement and the potential impact of these positions on Māori student learning; (2) to give voice to the participants (students, parents, principals, and teachers) in a manner that addressed power relations pertaining to issues of initiation, benefits, representation, legitimation and accountability; (3) in the professional development phase of the project, to provide teachers with a vicarious means of understanding how students experienced schooling in ways that they might not otherwise have access to in order to enable teachers to critically reflect upon their own discursive positioning and the impact this might have upon their own students' learning; and (4) to provide us with a practical representation of the theoretical model that was identified in the first part of this chapter.

Operationalizing a culturally effective pedagogy of relations in Aotearoa/ New Zealand means implementing the Effective Teaching Profile. This profile creates a learning context that is responsive to the culture of the child and means that learners can bring who they are to the classroom in complete safety and where their knowledges are acceptable and legitimate is central to this exercise. Such a context for learning stands in contrast to the traditional classroom where the culture of the teacher is given central focus and has the power to define what constitutes appropriate and acceptable knowledges, approaches to learning and understandings, and sense-making processes. This model suggests that when learners' own culture is central to learning activities, they are able to make meaning of new information and ideas by building on their own prior cultural experiences and understandings. The visible culture of the child need not necessarily be present but may well become present as a result of co-constructing learning experiences with teachers, in this way addressing the potential imposition of the teacher displaying cultural iconography. Such contexts for learning also teach learners how to critically reflect on their own learning, how they might learn better and more effectively, and ensure greater balance in the power relationship of learning by modeling this approach in class. In effect, therefore, raising expectations of students' own learning and how they might enhance and achieve these expectations engages students actively, holistically and in an integrated fashion, in real-life (or as close to) problem-sharing and questioning, and uses these questions as catalysts for ongoing study. This engagement can be monitored as an indicator of potential long-term achieve-ment. This shift from traditional classrooms is important because traditional classroom interaction patterns do not allow teachers to create learning con-texts where the culture of the child can be present, but rather assume cultural homogeneity (Villegas & Lucas, 2002), which in reality is cultural hegemony (Gay, 2010). Discursive classrooms have the potential to respond to Māori students and parents desires to 'be Māori,' desires that were made very clear in their narratives of experience. However it must be stressed that fundamen-tal to the development of discursive classrooms that include Māori students is the understanding that teachers' deficit theorizing must be challenged. Deficit theorizing will not be addressed unless there are more effective partnerships between Māori students and their teachers within the classrooms of mainstream schools. This understanding applies equally to those parenting Māori students. Once these aspects are addressed, the culture of the child can be brought to the learning context with all the power that has been hidden for so long.

The metaphors that Te Kotahitanga draws upon are holistic and flex-ible and able to be determined by or understood within the cultural contexts that have meaning to the lives of the many young people of diverse back-grounds who attend modern schools today. Teaching and learning strategies which flow from these metaphors are flexible and allow the diverse voices of young people primacy; they promote dialogue, communication and learning with others. In such a pedagogy, the participants in the learning interaction become involved in the process of collaboration—mutual storytelling and re-storying—so that a relationship can emerge in which both stories are heard, or indeed a process is established where a new story is created by all the par-ticipants. Such a pedagogy addresses Māori people's concerns about current pedagogic practices being fundamentally monocultural and epistemologically racist. This new pedagogy recognizes that all people who are involved in the learning and teaching process are participants who have meaningful experi-ences, valid concerns and legitimate questions.

This model constitutes the classroom as a place where young people's sense-making processes are incorporated and enhanced, where the existing knowledges of young people are seen as 'acceptable' and 'official,' in such a way that their stories provide the learning base from whence they can branch out into new fields of knowledge through structured interactions with significant others. In this process the teacher interacts with students in such a way that new knowledge is co-created. Such a classroom will generate totally different inter-action patterns and educational outcomes from a classroom where knowledge is seen as something that the teacher makes sense of and then passes on to students. The classroom will be conducted within and through a culturally responsive pedagogy of relations, wherein self-determining individuals interact with one another within non-dominating relations of interdependence.

Te Kotahitanga began in 2001 in a small way, and, as subsequent chapters of this book show, is beginning to make significant improvements in Māori student engagement with learning and achievement, along with major improvements in their enjoyment of the learning experience. Such an approach to creating learning contexts of course is not without its detractors, coming as it does from a once dominated and marginalized culture. Nevertheless, one of the main messages and challenges here for mainstream educators is as Freire (1972) identified above, that the answers to Māori educational achievement and disparities do not lie in the mainstream, for given the experiences of the last 150 years, mainstream practices and theories have kept Māori in a subordinate position, while at the same time creating a discourse that pathologized and marginalized Māori peoples' lived experiences.

The counter-narrative that is Kaupapa Māori demonstrates that the means of addressing the seemingly immutable educational disparities that plague Māori students in mainstream schools actually lies elsewhere than in mainstream education. The answers lie in the sense-making and knowledge-generating processes of the culture the dominant system has sought to marginalize for so long. The power of counter-narratives such as Kaupapa Māori, which has grown out of Māori resistance to the dominance of majority culture aspirations on our lives (G. Smith, 1997; L. Smith, 1999; Bishop, 1996), is such that alternative pedagogies that are both appropriate and responsive, can be developed out of the cultural sense-making processes of peoples previously marginalized by the dominance of colonial and neo-colonial educational relations of power. Such pedagogies can create learning contexts for previously pathologized and marginalized students in ways that allow them to participate in education on their terms, to be themselves and to achieve on their own terms as Māori as well as becoming, in Durie's (2002) terms, "citizens of the world".

· 3 ·

THE PROFESSIONAL DEVELOPMENT PROCESS

Mere Berryman, University of Waikato

As discussed in chapter 2, Te Kotahitanga is an iterative research and (professional) development (R&D) school reform program that is aimed at raising the achievement of New Zealand's indigenous Māori population through collaboration with school leaders and teachers to change classroom relationships and interactions. An Effective Teaching Profile, developed from the voices of Māori students and some of their teachers, provides focus for developing culturally responsive contexts for learning that are embedded in relationships of respect and interdependence. This same pedagogy provides the focus for the teacher and facilitator professional development.

This chapter begins by contextualising the professional development processes within the Effective Teaching Profile that emerged from the initial Te Kotahitanga research. It then sets out the cycle of professional development activities and some of the specific tools that are used at the level of preparing in-school facilitators to work with teachers. Using the voices of those engaged with the professional development, it also highlights the importance of pedagogies, in both professional development and classrooms, wherein self-determining individuals can use evidence to collaborate in the sharing and co-construction of new solutions towards their own response to raising Māori student achievement.

Background to the Professional Development

As discussed in Chapter 2, the overall aim of Te Kotahitanga was to improve the educational achievement of Māori students in secondary school class-rooms (Bishop et al., 2003). Te Kotahitanga began in 2001 when narratives of experience were collected from year 9 and 10 Māori students, their parents and other family members, their principals and some of their teachers (Bishop, & Berryman, 2006). From an analysis of unit ideas that was undertaken with these narratives, it emerged that a major influence on Māori students' educational achievement in schools lay in the minds and actions of their teachers (Bishop et al., 2003). The narratives of experience clearly identified that many teachers explained Māori students' educational achievement in terms of the students' deficiencies. These discourses ranged from students' lack of motivation, skills or abilities, to the perceived deficiencies within the students' homes. Others located the problem within the school's systems and structures. Teachers who were located in deficit discursive positions were unable to offer realistic solutions for improving the achievement levels of Māori students. Deficit theorising such as this appeared to lower teachers' expectations of Māori students, thus creating self-fulfilling prophesies of failure, and leaving many teachers frustrated about how to make a difference for Māori students. Teachers re-positioning within alternative, more agentic discourses, including their use of different pedagogy, was therefore seen to be a necessary condition for improving Māori student educational engagement and achievement. The sufficient condition, however, was in the provision of an institutionalised and ongoing means for teachers to collaboratively reflect upon their practice and change in light of a range of evidence of Māori students' participation and achievement. The professional development in Te Kotahitanga has been an iterative response to these two conditions identified from the research findings, iterative in the sense that it applies the Research, Implementation, Development, and Evaluation (RIDE) model.

The narratives of experience from Māori students clearly articulated their concerns about the majority of teaching practices in relation to themselves. However, these students, and some of their teachers, also clearly articulated pedagogy that would engage them more effectively with learning in the class-room. These suggestions were then aligned with the current literature on effective teaching which in turn led to the development of the Te Kotahitanga Effective Teaching Profile (Bishop et al., 2003) seen in Chapter 2.

Te Kotahitanga researchers found that fundamental to the Effective Teaching Profile was the need to challenge teachers to explicitly reject deficit theorizing as a means of explaining the disparity in Māori students' educational achievement levels, and instead to take a position of agency in their own theorizing and practice. That is, teachers would express their own professional commitment, responsibility and ability to bring about change in Māori students' educational achievement by accepting their own professional responsibility for the learning outcomes of these students. These two central understandings (reject deficit theorizing as a means to explaining disparity and take responsibility for what you can achieve professionally) are then manifested by teachers on a daily basis in their classroom pedagogy, through relationships and interactions that demonstrate that they care for and understand Māori students as culturally located individuals; that they have high expectations for Māori students' learning and behavior; that they manage their classroom pedagogy so as to promote Māori students' engagement with learning; that they promote a wider range of learning interactions with Māori students by incorporating interactive strategies to facilitate engagement with learning; and that they promote, monitor and reflect upon their Māori students' learning outcomes in ways that lead to improvements in achievement. Teachers then share these successes with Māori students and their home communities which in turn, promotes further success (Bishop et al., 2003; Bishop & Berryman, 2006).

The implementation of learning contexts such as those described in the Effective Teaching Profile have since seen many teachers and facilitators in Te Kotahitanga begin to generate what the research team have termed a Culturally Responsive Pedagogy of Relations:

> where power is shared between self-determining individuals within non-dominating relations of interdependence; where culture counts; where pedagogy is interactive, dialogic and spirals; where participants are connected to one another through the establishment of a common vision for what constitutes excellence in educational outcomes. (Bishop, Berryman, Cavanagh, & Teddy, 2007, p. 25)

The Effective Teaching Profile and the subsequent creation of culturally responsive contexts provide the direction and focus for the pedagogy, both in the classrooms of teachers participating in Te Kotahitanga, and in the professional development undertaken with these teachers and facilitators.

This professional development provides the institutionalized and ongoing means to collaboratively reflect upon teaching practices and student evidence in order to work for school-wide reform. Teachers who involve themselves with culturally responsive pedagogy attempt to create contexts whereby learners can bring their own cultural knowledge and experiences to the learning as the basis for actively constructing new knowledge with others (Bruner, 1996). Contexts such as these are more likely to involve learning in and through the culture of the student with the student able to determine and direct his or her own learning. Such contexts require relationships of trust and interdependence amongst students and teachers if sharing and learning is to flourish. The term "culturally responsive pedagogy" is often used interchangeably with "critical pedagogy" (Freire, 1976), where the central tenet positions both the teacher and learners simultaneously as learners and teachers. That is, the teacher can be both the teacher and at times the learner and students respectively can be both the learner and teacher. Contexts such as these align strongly with the Māori process of 'ako' as discussed in New Zealand by Pere (1994). The word "ako" represents the interdependent nature of the roles of teacher and learner as being both to teach (kaiako) and to learn (akonga). Those who use culturally responsive pedagogy of relations accept the cultural location of all learners; they also accept that the success of this pedagogy is embedded in the relationships that exist between teachers and learners, and between learners and learners. Rather than imposing their own culture upon learners, teachers learn about the lives of learners in other settings and they create contexts whereby learners can bring their own experiences into the settings where teaching and learning takes place (Bishop, Berryman, Powell, & Teddy, 2007; Bishop & Glynn, 1999; Bruner, 1996; Villegas & Lucas, 2002).

School-Based Facilitation Teams

Each school that participates in Te Kotahitanga forms a facilitation team that includes the principal and a number of facilitators. The principal's leadership in promoting and participating in teacher professional development is understood to have a demonstrable impact on participating teachers as well as on student achievement (Robinson, 2007). One of the core tasks of Senior Management within participating Te Kotahitanga schools is their own selection of facilitators and the establishment and configuration of facilitation teams.

Facilitators are selected from experienced classroom practitioners, some of whom are existing members of staff released from their teaching duties, and others who are external to the school (school advisors and resource teachers). Initial Ministry funding ensures that schools have one full-time staffing component for every 30 teachers in Te Kotahitanga. A lead facilitator is supported by one or more additional facilitators; the total percentage of FTE for the team is determined based on student and teacher numbers. At a typical medium-size school, in addition to the lead facilitator, there are part-time facilitators who spend their remaining time in a variety of instructional roles either as teachers in the school or travelling to other schools for teaching-related work. Over the years, as Ministry funding is withdrawn, providing sufficient capacity within the team to fully support the teachers in the program has been one of the biggest challenges.

Facilitators engage in an ongoing working relationship with members of the Te Kotahitanga Research and Development (R&D) team in preparation for their facilitation of all Te Kotahitanga related professional development activities with teachers in their own schools. Experienced facilitators learn to support teachers in a term-by-term cycle that involves four components:

1. Classroom observations to monitor and reflect on their classroom pedagogy; observations provide specific feedback on the degree to which teachers are incorporating pedagogy based on relationships and interactions from the Effective Teaching Profile into their practice.
2. Individual feedback and goal setting
3. Co-construction in which groups of teachers use evidence from students' learning to co-construct group goals
4. Shadow-coaching, in which facilitators negotiate with teachers then provide the coaching support required in order that teachers can achieve the goals that have been set.

This cycle ensures ongoing opportunities, for critical reflection and feedback, based on the gathering and shared reflections on student evidence.

The Professional Development for Facilitators

The Te Kotahitanga R&D team provide ongoing professional development to every person identified by schools as part of their facilitation team. Despite individual facilitators entering Te Kotahitanga with different prior knowledge and experiences, the professional development tries to be responsive to all participants. The professional development of facilitators begins with an induction hui (a meeting conducted within Māori cultural protocols) that opens with the R&D team and the facilitators participating in Māori culturally located rituals of encounter that involve making connections to each other and to the Te Kotahitanga agenda. Each subsequent professional development hui begins by renewing relationships and reconnecting. This process of making connections and developing relationships, known by Māori as whakawhanaungatanga, is integral to the trust that develops between the R&D team and facilitators. Just as teachers' relationships with Māori students provide a classroom context within which students are encouraged to bring their own prior knowledge and experiences to their learning, relationships and the application and sharing of one's own prior knowledge and expertise, are the foundation upon which the professional development is built.

Professional development hui

At the first hui, the facilitators are introduced to the theorising underpinning Te Kotahitanga, the pedagogy of the Effective Teaching Profile and the specific elements of practice that will be the focus of their own work in providing professional development for teachers in their own schools. Facilitators learn how to use the Te Kotahitanga Observation Tool (described later in this chapter) and to facilitate the four components of the in-school cycle of professional development that will constitute their core facilitation tasks. Immediately after the first hui, facilitation teams are expected to use the observation tool to undertake baseline observations in the classroom of each teacher who has volunteered to participate in the program. Baseline observations are carried out with shadow coaching support from members of the R&D team who review these observation practices from school to school. These processes ensure that facilitators are using the observation tool with at least an 80% inter-observer level of reliability. At the second hui facilitators learn how to introduce Te Kotahitanga to their first cohort of 30 teachers who have volunteered to be in the program.

Each professional development hui involves at least three days of intensive information sharing, modeling and reflection. The pedagogies used in the professional development model the Effective Teaching Profile. They include traditional transmission interactions (instruction/modeling: monitoring; feedback and feed-forward on behavior) where the learner is largely seen as the apprentice (Rogoff, 1990), and continue through to interactions that promote the construction of knowledge where learners are understood as active agents in their own learning (use of prior knowledge and experiences; feedback and feed-forward on academic learning; and co-construction). The R&D team model the procedures required for introducing teachers to Te Kotahitanga, as well as supporting and monitoring teachers throughout the processes of change. For many this involves new pedagogies that promote a model of 'developing expertise' rather than a focus on being the 'expert'. These processes model the activities that facilitators will be engaged with in their schools, using the pedagogies within the Effective Teacher Profile, so that facilitators can first engage with and then pass these activities and pedagogies on more effectively to their teachers.

Following the two induction hui run by the R&D team, facilitators begin Te Kotahitanga in their own schools by running their own induction hui with their first cohort of teachers. This hui is modelled on the one that they themselves have attended and, in the first instance, it is undertaken with shadow coaching support from at least one person from the R&D team. After facilitating the induction hui with teachers, facilitators then begin to implement the cycle of four Te Kotahitanga in-class activities with teachers (observation, feedback, co-construction meetings and shadow coaching). After having all activities modelled, ongoing support to hone their skills and to relate new ideas and theorising to practice continues to be provided to facilitators by a member of the R&D team. As discussed, the R&D support begins by modelling all activities to facilitation teams. It then follows a cycle of first shadow-coaching (acting as a guide on the side) the lead facilitator on each activity the first time it is implemented and then in the second cycle, as a reviewer of the facilitator's practices. In this way, the lead facilitator is then supported to conduct these same shadow-coaching and reviewing activities with every member of their team.

The shadow-coaching is used as the basis for learning conversations that connect facilitators to their own work of making a difference for teachers, who in turn will be better placed to make a difference for their Māori students. Professional development such as this provides a research and development model that is iterative and dynamic and where the power-sharing relationships of trust that have been established between members of the R&D team and facilitators, form the basis of ongoing interactions.

At the end of the first term's implementation of the in-school cycle of professional development with teachers, the third annual national hui for facilitation teams is held. These national professional development hui, and the smaller regional professional development hui, are facilitated by the R&D team. Together, with the regular R&D team school visits, these hui provide ongoing opportunities for facilitation teams to engage in collaborative, critical reflection on their practice in working with teachers to raise the achievement of Māori students within their own schools.

The themes for the national hui always emerge from what has been happening in schools, either what schools have been doing or what they want or need to know. Each hui follow a similar pattern and involve a number of key components. As already identified, they always begin with whakawhanaungatanga, the renewal of relationships to each other, to the goal and to the purpose of the hui. Following this there is always a time to discuss what has been happening in schools and to set down any *burning questions* or *gnarly issues*. Later in the hui an activity to collaboratively problem solve the gnarly issues sees the collective wisdom of the group contributing authentic solutions to their own problems. Hui usually involve one or two plenary sessions, where new learning around the theme of the hui is presented. They also contain a session to develop or maintain new knowledge. In these sessions facilitators share their own perspectives in order to consolidate the specific new knowledge and themes. These sessions are always followed by multiple activities, using a range of templates and/or schema, to promote discussion, gather reflections and take their learning deeper. Stock-take exercises in school teams allow facilitators to align the new learning and knowledge with their own theories and practice and also to reflect on the possible implications to their work in schools. Hui always conclude with a planning session that challenges facilitators to incorporate new understandings into a coherent plan for their return to schools.

Resource Developments

A number of Te Kotahitanga resources have been developed to support facilitators' professional learning. These resources are aimed at providing facilitators with resources that can be used in their implementation of the professional development cycle within their schools. They include a number of DVD resources that focus on teachers' interactions and relationships within the Effective Teaching Profile, as well as facilitators modeling and theorizing their practices of Feedback, Co-construction and Shadow-coaching. They also include a number of reference manuals or short modules that have been developed as for each of the core Te Kotahitanga activities in schools. Other professional development activities that support Te Kotahitanga, such as new teaching strategies and/or assessment procedures are introduced as facilitators identify a need at a classroom level. Many of these resources can now be accessed from the Te Kotahitanga website at http://tekotahitanga.tki.org.nz/

The Professional Development for Teachers

The first component of professional development for participating teachers is the induction hui that introduces each new cohort of teachers to the basic tenets of Te Kotahitanga. These hui are usually held at a local marae (a traditional Māori cultural meeting place) with Māori elders present and actively engaged in the professional development. The marae provides a culturally appropriate setting where Māori as the majority culture is *normal*. Holding these annual induction hui on marae opens up ongoing lines of communication between schools and the elders and parents of their local Māori community. As each new group of teachers is included into the project, schools have the opportunity to demonstrate their commitment to their local Māori community, and to signal that they are seriously engaged in addressing the educational achievement of their Māori students.

At the hui, teachers are introduced to the need of addressing the specific goal of raising Māori student participation and achievement. Māori students' experiences of education (and those of their families) are then worked through in a problem-solving exercise using the original narratives of experience (Bishop & Berryman, 2006). This provides teachers with an opportunity to critically examine their own discursive positioning and its implications for their own classroom relations and interactions with Māori students. Through this process, teachers are invited to critically reflect upon the evidence presented in the narratives of Māori students and others. A professional learning conversation is created wherein teachers can critically reflect upon their own experiences in similar settings. This activity provides opportunities for teachers to begin to identify and challenge their own discursive positioning. Teachers are invited to reject deficit thinking (". . . *until something happens for this family, there is nothing I can do*", ". . . *these Māori students are just not up to it*"), and pathologizing practices (". . . *they need more remedial work, special*

programs, they can't cope with this work") as a means to theorizing Māori student achievement levels. They begin to understand how they themselves can
operate more effectively from a position of agency (*"maybe I can't do anything
about this child's home circumstances but in my classroom, I can do. . ."*).

This process of challenging teachers' explanations and practices (repositioning within alternative discourses) about what impacts on Māori students'
learning, provides teachers with the opportunity to challenge their own deficit
theorizing about Māori students (and their communities) through real and
vicarious means and in ways that are non-confrontational. It is a fundamental
understanding of Te Kotahitanga that until teachers consider how the dominant culture maintains control over the various aspects of education, and the
part they themselves might play in perpetuating this pattern of domination,
albeit unwittingly, they will not understand how dominance manifests itself
in the lives of Māori students and how they as teachers, in the way they relate
to and interact with Māori students, may well be affecting learning in their
classroom. Therefore, the professional development devised by the researchers
maintains a means whereby teachers' thinking can be challenged, albeit in a
respectful and supported way. Cognitive and affective dissonance, in effect,
cultural dissonance, which Timperley et al. (2003) identify as being necessary
for successful professional development, can lead teachers to a better understanding of the power imbalances of which they are a part, in particular, those
power imbalances which perpetuate cultural deficit theorizing and support the
retention of traditional transmission classroom practices.

The professional development induction hui then turns to examine the
relationships that are exemplified when teachers care for students, have high
expectations of them and manage learning in classrooms using more discursive
and interactive pedagogies that are fundamental to creating culturally responsive contexts for learning. Strategies that can be used to develop relations of
care and in-class learning conversations are specifically introduced next, and
indeed are also used as the model for presentation throughout the professional
development hui with teachers. The importance of detailed planning to bring
about change in classrooms, in departments and across the school is then identified and discussed.

In-school cycle of professional development activities

Following the induction hui, teachers begin the term-by-term cycle of observation, feedback, co-construction and shadow-coaching. Once a term (four

times a year), a facilitator conducts a classroom observation with each participating teacher. Observations are followed soon after by an individual, specific
feedback meeting. During the feedback meeting, the facilitator and the teacher
deconstruct and discuss the evidence recorded during the observed lesson.
This discussion is focussed on the degree to which the teacher is implementing
the Effective Teaching Profile in his or her classroom practice. Together, the
facilitator and the teacher construct new directions for future pedagogy and,
from the evidence and feedback, they collaboratively develop an individual
teacher goal.

Teachers then participate in a facilitated group co-construction meeting
where they are encouraged to set a common group goal, this time focused on
enhancing their group's implementation of the Effective Teaching Profile.
Ideally, Te Kotahitanga co-construction meetings are cross-curricular and
include a group of teachers who teach a common group of students. Following
co-construction meetings, facilitators provide shadow-coaching to support
teachers to achieve their set goals.

This term-by-term cycle (observation, individual feedback, group co-construction and shadow coaching) forms the basis of the in-school professional
development program. This cycle ensures that there are ongoing opportunities for reflection and feedback based on the accurate and objective gathering of classroom evidence for summative and formative purposes. Thus, new
pedagogical understandings are determined by a shared understanding of the
implications of a range of classroom evidence together with teachers' and
facilitator's experiential knowledge.

The Te Kotahitanga Observation Tool

The Te Kotahitanga Observation Tool provides the framework for monitoring
the degree to which participating teachers are incorporating the relationships
and interactions from the Effective Teaching Profile into their everyday teaching. Using this tool, the impact of teachers' pedagogy on Māori students can be
reliably observed by an experienced observer (Bishop, Berryman, Cavanagh,
& Lamont, 2007). The specific evidence from observations is then fed back
to individual teachers by the observer/facilitator, after which new understandings are co-jointly constructed as the basis for an ongoing cycle of professional
development.

The developers of the Te Kotahitanga Observation Tool acknowledge
that there are many factors within the learning environment that contribute to

students' behaviour and learning. Observations that focus on students alone are likely to be located within a functional limitations paradigm (Moore et al., 1999) that suggests the problem or deficiency is found within the student. In contrast to this paradigm, the development of the Te Kotahitanga Observation Tool draws upon understandings from both kaupapa Māori and socio-cultural perspectives on human learning (Rogoff, 1990; Vygotsky, 1978). Kaupapa Māori perspectives emphasise the importance of relationships that are collective and relational and, at the same time, set high expectations that are mutually responsive and evolving. Socio-cultural perspectives emphasise the responsive social and cultural contexts in which learning takes place as being key components to successful learning (Glynn, Wearmouth, & Berryman, 2006; Gregory, 1996; Rogoff, 1990; Vygotsky, 1978). Socio-cultural perspectives highlight the acquisition of knowledge and skills through social interactions, in formal and informal settings. Contextualised social interactions such as these are also increasingly seen as fundamental to the acquisition of intellectual knowledge and skills (Bronfenbrenner, 1979; Bruner, 1996; McNaughton, 2002).

Important information therefore may be attained by taking into account what can be learned from the direct observation of teachers and students in authentic responsive, social settings such as are encouraged through the implementation of the Effective Teaching Profile. In these settings it is possible for the teacher to implement strategies that will promote a responsive and interactive role where students have opportunities to exercise a measure of autonomy in their learning and where teachers may assume a facilitative and constructive role in relation to the development of knowledge, rather than a solely directive, transmission role. Thus, within the Effective Teaching Profile, knowledge is understood to be both constructed as well as transmitted. The breadth of these observation parameters therefore is an attempt to provide greater scope for examining evidence that will generate a range of effective and meaningful solutions for teachers and Māori students while at the same time, be inclusive of all other students.

To reiterate, this observation tool facilitates gathering evidence of teachers' implementation of the Effective Teaching Profile. It provides the framework for classroom observations and is focused on gathering evidence about teachers' classroom relationships and interactions with Māori students.

The tool is on two sides of paper. Side one is used to objectively gather and quantify evidence of teaching and learning interactions between teachers and Māori students within authentic, teaching and learning settings. Side two gathers evidence of the relationships between teachers and Māori students in these same settings.

Evidence of the teaching and learning interactions observed using side one of the observation tool includes the teachers':

- description of the lesson;
- level of cognitive challenge of the lesson for the specific class of students being observed;
- range of pedagogical interactions used with students, from pedagogy that is traditional transmission to that which is more interactive and constructive;
- direct interactions with student groupings, from whole class, small group or individual student; and
- location throughout the observation.

Side one is also used to gather evidence about the lesson from five Māori students that includes their:

- engagement with the lesson;
- work completion, in line with expectations observed to have been set by the teacher; and
- location throughout the observation.

Finally side one is also used to gather any other relevant information about the teacher, the lesson or the class in order to add richness to the observation information.

Side two of the observation tool is used to gather evidence about:

- the teacher's relationships with Māori students;
- the teacher's expectations of Māori students' learning and behaviour;
- visible signs of culture in the classroom;
- cultural responsiveness of the teaching context to Māori students; and
- strategies being used by the teacher.

Accurate use of the Te Kotahitanga Observation tool, by facilitators trained in the observation conventions, allows teachers to share in the process of monitoring and reflecting on their own Effective Teaching Profile practice through a facilitated cycle of observation followed by individual feedback.

Individual teacher feedback

The information from observations then enables observers (the facilitators) to provide teachers with specific feedback and feed-forward on observed teacher-student learning expectations, interactions, and strategies as well as the impact of these interactions on five Māori students in terms of their engagement and work completion.

At previously negotiated times following the classroom observations, facilitators give teachers specific feedback about the lesson they have formally observed using the observation tool. Teachers talk with their facilitators about their recent in-class experiences with Māori students and begin to co-construct new directions in terms of individual goals for future teaching. Facilitators avoid general feedback but instead consider seven types of specific feedback: feedback on what was observed; feedback to reflect; opportunities for teachers to feedback; feedback on relationships; positive feedback; feedback to move teachers forward in their practice (feed-forward); and responsive feedback. Facilitators also ensure that feedback sessions are based specifically on the events recorded or annotated during the classroom observation and conclude with reminders or links to their next co-construction meeting.

Teachers' feedback sessions normally take 40 minutes to an hour and in the early stages of the project consist of feedback being given to the teacher by the facilitator. However, as the teachers become familiar with the observation data and the interrelatedness of the various components observed, these sessions become much more interactive. Indeed, from their initial observation and across subsequent observations, it is evident that teachers may well be undergoing a developmental continuum of responses to their own observation data. As will be shown in Chapter 5, the first response is usually for teachers to be rather passive and receptive of the data, what it shows and what it might mean for their practice. At this stage, teachers generally see student engagement and work completion as separate outcomes. The second response is seen when teachers begin to understand for themselves what the interrelated data show and seek advice about how they might change their practice in relation to student engagement and work completion. The third response is where the teacher and facilitator become co-constructors of the knowledge that is created from the observation tool, and the meanings of the relationships between the students' outcomes and their practice. In other words, through this process of facilitated feedback, learning conversations develop to a stage where the teacher is more likely to take the lead in the analysis of the data and to seek suggestions and co-construct solutions with the facilitator as to how they might go about developing caring relationships in the classroom. At this point, teachers are well placed to change classroom interactions in order to improve Māori student outcomes in their classrooms in terms of Māori student engagement, work completion, attendance and achievement. It is worth noting that through the use of evidence and co-constructing the teacher's next steps, the facilitation team is modelling through this process the means whereby the teacher can improve the participation and engagement of Māori students in the classroom. Facilitators ensure that the teachers feel at ease and understand that what is discussed in their individual feedback sessions is confidential and will not be shared with others unless they choose to share these things themselves. We have been clear that these observations should not be seen, in any way, as related to teacher appraisal.

The co-construction meeting

The co-construction meetings are facilitated, problem-solving opportunities for a group of teachers to collaboratively reflect on evidence and co-construct solutions. Ideally, co-construction groups are made up of teachers who come from different curriculum areas, yet who work with a common group of students. The focus of co-construction meetings is for teachers to collaboratively examine evidence of Māori (and other) students' participation and progress with learning. This activity is undertaken in order to collaboratively develop plans and strategies that will further promote each of the elements of the Effective Teaching Profile in their classrooms, in order to improve Māori students' educational experiences and thus lead to measurable improvements in participation and achievement.

Facilitators again work to ensure that teachers know that co-construction meetings are not linked to performance appraisal, nor designed to demean or to glorify individuals, but rather they are aimed at improving Māori student achievement. Facilitators emphasize that the co-construction process is about working collaboratively towards improving or maintaining positive relationships with Māori students and moving towards using more culturally responsive and discursive teaching and learning interactions in their classrooms. The teachers in the co-construction group are given space to reflect upon and share evidence collected as a result of their classroom practice. Such evidence may come from a range of sources including students' participation, their achievement and progress with learning, attendance patterns, students' actual work, teacher-developed pre- and post-test data or data from standardized norm-referenced tests. Co-construction meetings conclude by setting times and dates with the facilitator for shadow coaching to further support the implementation of their newly set goals.

Shadow coaching

Shadow coaching involves the facilitator supporting individual teachers to meet their personal and group goals by coaching them in their classroom or other setting where work towards the goal is naturally likely to occur. This might involve collaboratively planning lessons, making adaptations to the learning environment or curriculum, or physically modeling steps towards the goal. It is likely to involve giving the teacher another opportunity for feedback and reflection on observed classroom interactions. Facilitators are expected to negotiate specific times and processes with teachers. Facilitators understand that they may have to provide shadow-coaching a number of times to ensure that the goals are being met.

The Leadership Professional Development

Each year, one of the national professional development hui specifically focuses on the leadership of the reform in schools. An example was one held for principals and lead facilitators from 12 schools that began Te Kotahitanga in 2001, after they had been part of Te Kotahitanga for three years. The focus of the first sessions was on reporting back Māori student evidence, both from the schools themselves and from the R&D team. This was followed by collective, co-construction as to what *Stepping up to Sustainability* meant for the participants in their role as the leaders of Te Kotahitanga within their own schools. Each school was asked to give a brief presentation detailing their own implementation and results from Te Kotahitanga. Following the schools' presentations and the sharing of student and teacher evidence from the R&D team, there were facilitated opportunities for joint, critical reflection, within and across school teams, on the implications of the evidence for the sustainability of Te Kotahitanga in their own schools.

Within these professional learning conversations (Timperly, Phillips, & Wiseman, 2003), principals and lead facilitators continued the critical reflection on their own school's evidence to co-construct the pathway ahead. Remaining team members joined the hui on the second day. Facilitated opportunities to share and reflect critically on the evidence and its implications, continued within and across teams. This particular hui culminated in an examination of components required for sustaining school reform (Bishop, O'Sullivan, & Berryman, 2010) and schools' planning their own specific next steps forward. The use of school-based evidence at this hui provided facilitators and principals with supported opportunities to critically reflect on their own evidence and apply their experiences and expertise to problem solving around the common vision of what constitutes excellence in educational outcomes for Māori students in their schools and how this will be increased and maintained.

Feedback and reflections from this hui showed that for every comment that celebrated the interactive professional development opportunities that had been provided, there was someone else who felt challenged by, or even daunted by the new activities. On the one hand, feedback highlighted the continuum of experience and expertise within Te Kotahitanga school teams. On the other hand, feedback also indicated the importance of the relationships and expectations that had been built up over time between these 12 school teams and members of the R&D team. Responses were honest and from the heart, often hard hitting yet respectful, clearly expecting that the R&D team would continue to be responsive and available to schools.

Reflecting on the Model of Professional Development

Professional development activities within Te Kotahitanga have resulted in a professional development model that in many respects replicates the Effective Teaching Profile being applied by Te Kotahitanga teachers in classrooms. The following quotes from facilitators come from their evaluations of Te Kotahitanga professional development activities. One lead facilitator suggested:

> The . . . professional development hui have been exemplary in terms of helping us to support our teachers. They have been well paced, resourced and they have modelled co-construction, in fact the Effective Teaching Profile.

At each hui, facilitators who have participated in the professional development have been quick to take an agentic position, focussing on what they can do and in the main showing a huge commitment to learning how to bring about change in order to support the educational achievement of Māori students. Those that stay in agentic positions learn the importance of developing strong relationships with other people in the project and commit to the challenging task of bringing about school-wide reform. The relationships that are developed are based on a strong commitment and belief in the common goal of raising Māori students' achievement and a common understanding that what we can do interdependently is more powerful than what any one of us can do independently (Berryman, Glynn, Togo, & McDonald, 2004). The following lead facilitator likens this to being part of a family.

> To be in Te Kotahitanga is a lifetime commitment. Okay we're not just going on a course . . . and then coming home and being left to ourselves. Being in Te Kotahitanga we're part of the community and we've got the support of each other. . . . You have got that community group. Also we've got like Auntie Nan [Māori elder who acts as a cultural advisor] on one level you know that's quite important for me and we've got [the R&D team] at the next level and then us, so it truly is a family and we're not left to do things on our own. And so all of our ideas, all of our experiences are valued and that's what has happened in the last couple of years.

Just as teachers in Te Kotahitanga classrooms are encouraged to develop relationships of trust and care with Māori students, through their implementation of the professional development activities, members of the R&D team attempt to develop the same relationships with the school leaders and Te Kotahitanga facilitators with whom they work.

> Our team felt strengthened by the increase in knowledge and strategies role modelled to us by the [R&D] team. Every hui was a chance to rejuvenate the batteries and enthusiasm—it served to centre us again on the right course. Many thanks for that.

> Without the training there would be no ETP for us to support. The training [has] been invaluable. The time to talk with others has also been of significant value.

Relationships such as these are able to support a professional development model that utilizes the same Effective Teaching Profile that is being used by Te Kotahitanga teachers, where pedagogical interactions involve the school leaders and Te Kotahitanga facilitators in both the transmission and co-construction of new knowledge.

The first couple of hui that I went to . . . I felt like I was stood down and all this stuff was bombarding me and I needed to take it away and spend three weeks on an island to digest it. I remember saying to people I just want time to sit down and be able to talk about this and kind of get my head around this and soak it in. But there wasn't that time, it was like right we've only got three days and like get set, go.

Although beginning on this pathway can be quite daunting for some, others talk about the professional development as a journey, where expertise is shared and all contributions are valued and respected. They soon learn that what is talked about and incorporated into the professional development hui is what they will be encouraging teachers to do in their classrooms with students.

We've come out of a hierarchal model and it takes [time], you just can't go from one island to another and suddenly belong there. We actually have to lose those traits and develop these new ones so this has been part of the journey. So looking back you can say you need to start off in that way [transmission pedagogy] but as people you need that opportunity to develop the ability to sit in a group of people and know you are going to collaborate, you are going to have shared expertise, you are going to value and respect everybody because that's how we function.

Rather than being solely a transmission model of professional development driven by an outside expert, this model of professional development is based on the understanding that all participating individuals bring particular skills and expertise with them and learning can actively ensue from the conversations that are had with each other.

We are there facilitating those sorts of interactions and we are encouraging teachers to have those interactions in the classrooms and so it makes perfect sense to be living it but I do say that it takes time to get there just like those teachers.

The ongoing group discussions with other facilitators [are] very helpful, either by affirming what we are doing or learning from them and by verbalising our thinking, we deepen our understanding.

When learning contexts are developed where each individual is able to contribute expertise for the collective benefit of the whole group, everybody learns. Facilitators bring expertise related to the implementation of Te Kotahitanga within their own schools and the R&D team brings expertise emerging from a research perspective, a view across schools, and knowledge of the changes over time. In the words of the following lead facilitator, this professional development is about relationships amongst people and not about being provided with just a "box of tricks."

... it's about dealing with people. .... You know everybody sharing and bringing in
their own cultural perspectives, spirituality and those other things. Other professional
development things you go [to], you pick up your box of tricks and you take them
back. You might as well go and buy a book and try and work it out because there is
no personal connection in it.

Feedback such as this is consistent across the professional development
hui. For example facilitators at one of the day-long regional hui highlighted
the importance of being able to bring issues and questions to share across the
teams. They also highlighted the importance of the learning conversations
that ensued and the co-construction opportunities that these hui offered in
order to plan the way forward.

> Good to go over issues with others, sharing opinions. Good to know issues at this
> stage are common to many schools and some common issues are being considered by
> project team also.
>
> Always good to have the 'big picture' conversations which often get lost in the day to
> day 'doing'. Also to share ideas, problems, solutions with other teams. A good spring-
> board for re-invigorated conversations within our own team back at school.

Feedback also indicate that the iterative nature of the Research,
Implementation, Development, Evaluation (RIDE) model being applied within
the Te Kotahitanga project, was valued by school-based facilitators.

> Good to get the feedback—showed me how to read the info and what I should be
> looking at in my school including improvements to our current systems.
>
> ... feedback on data was excellent and interesting—also should promote very inter-
> esting discussions within our school. Great results too as having clear cut data which
> supports our work is warmly welcomed.

As with other hui, it continues to be clear from feedback, that the use of
school-based evidence is an essential part of the professional development and
that the professional expertise within the schools' facilitation teams is just as
important as the expertise within the R&D team. It is also clear that the conversations that are started at these professional development hui continue back
in schools where others are able to bring their expertise into the conversation as
well. This is a professional development model where questions and issues came
from within the group and where this is seen as acceptable and indeed encouraged; where evidence is interrogated; where learning is in the conversations; and
where sometimes we are the learner and sometimes we are the teacher.

Conclusion

As suggested by Bishop and Glynn (1999) and by Bishop, Berryman, Powell and Teddy (2007), this model of professional development is one that creates power-sharing contexts wherein self-determining individuals work together to both share and construct new knowledge. Evidence is used for both summative and formative purposes, allowing those involved to reflect on outcomes with the express purpose of determining the next best steps and setting new goals that will support this to happen. The ongoing evidence generated from the work in schools forms the basis of the professional development program. Regular scheduled professional development activities provide opportunities for critical reflection on the cycle of observation, feedback, co-construction and shadow coaching undertaken by school-based Te Kotahitanga facilitators. This cycle continues to ensure that there are ongoing opportunities for reflection and feedback based on the accurate and objective gathering and mutual sharing of evidence, followed by the setting of new goals with which to redefine the way ahead for raising the achievement of Māori students.

· 4 ·

EVALUATING THE EFFECTIVENESS AND IMPACT OF TEACHER PROFESSIONAL DEVELOPMENT

Luanna H. Meyer, Victoria University

Introduction

The intended focus and purpose of a professional development program determine which outcomes are relevant to an evaluation of its effectiveness and impact. If teacher professional development is designed to change teacher attitudes or specific teacher practices, evaluation requires documentation of impact of the professional development activities on those attitudes or practices. Ultimately, the purpose of teacher professional development activities is to enhance achievement (or other) outcomes for students. Demonstrating changes in student outcomes as a function of teacher professional development is, however, complicated given the many factors other than actions by teachers that also influence student achievement—both positive and negative. Appropriate evaluation is not always straightforward, even where there is agreement regarding which student outcomes are expected to change as a function of teacher change and with respect to how to measure those student outcomes. Hattie's (2009) meta-analysis shows that teachers do have a major impact on student outcomes; nevertheless the link between teacher change and student outcomes is complex. Teacher influences become even more challenging to examine once students reach secondary school, where each student is exposed to instruction by multiple teachers across different subjects each year. In New Zealand, a typical high school student will be taught by up to 20 different teachers across the final three years of high school. Hence, evaluating individual student outcomes as a function of teacher professional development is complicated, requiring data from multiple perspectives.

Teacher professional development designed to achieve specific outcomes may also be affected by lack of competence in other, relevant skill areas that can either hinder or facilitate the acquisition and mastery of new content. In Te Kotahitanga, the major focus of the professional development is teacher development in the use of culturally responsive pedagogies across the curriculum. Whether or not teachers acquire new skills and understandings in culturally responsive pedagogies will be affected by what teachers already know and do. If a particular teacher lacks basic subject matter knowledge and/or has major shortcomings in classroom management, it would be unrealistic to expect teacher education focused on culturally responsive pedagogies to remedy these kinds of underlying problems and skill deficits. In such cases, failure to master culturally responsive pedagogies may simply reflect the absence of important, basic teacher competencies already undermining teaching and learning in the classroom.

Evaluation research is also affected by contextual realities. It may be virtually impossible to impose rigorous experimental design standards to investigate effectiveness and impact. For example, the recommended random assignment to intervention and control groups is unlikely in the real world of schools. Alternative quasi-experimental designs may need to be adapted to allow appropriate comparisons between schools with and without an innovative new program. Variations across schools can affect decisions regarding methodological approaches and outcome measures, and there may be additional practical limitations regarding the logistics and timeframes affecting availability of evidence about intended outcomes.

Scope of the evaluation

This chapter describes the evaluation approach and research design methodologies used by the independent evaluation team to investigate the effectiveness and impact of Te Kotahitanga as a school-wide, large-scale teacher professional development program. The ultimate purpose of Te Kotahitanga is the enhancement of Māori student educational outcomes, but other variables needed to be included in the evaluation to assess progress towards this goal. The enhancement of student achievement as an outcome attributable to Te Kotahitanga requires evidence that teachers understand, value, and implement culturally responsive pedagogies effectively as a function of program activities—beyond good teaching generally. To document effectiveness, the evaluation investigated the impact of Te Kotahitanga at the various different levels expected to be affected by the program, including evidence for the acquisition of new skills and understandings by teachers. Interestingly, as noted in Chapter 1, there is currently sparse empirical evidence in the published literature regarding effective teacher education strategies to ensure that teachers understand and use culturally responsive pedagogies. Most of what has been published in this area over the past two to three decades is theory-based and values-driven, grounded primarily in logical argument. Even specific program descriptions typically report only participant satisfaction data such as whether the teachers enjoyed the professional development activities and believed they were worthwhile. There are also a few small-scale case studies reporting anecdotal information analyzed qualitatively. Overall, the literature reveals a dearth of empirically validated evaluation research that documents teacher or student behavior change outcomes as a function of teacher education and professional development activities.

Empirically, then, documentation of behavior change outcomes for teachers and students as a function of teacher education activities to master culturally responsive pedagogical practices represents a relatively new challenge. This makes it appropriate to incorporate investigation of a range of potentially relevant variables in the evaluation, though we privileged some information. For example, professional development program descriptions typically include teacher self-reports of satisfaction with the activities and program. We considered that such reports have limited utility. They are most likely to be useful as part of formative (not summative) evaluation in order to refine professional development activities; teacher satisfaction is in fact quite distant from the intended goal of enhanced student outcomes. Thus, teacher satisfaction with the Te Kotahitanga program per se was not of direct interest to the summative evaluation, although teacher self-reports about the impact of the program on their own understandings, knowledge, and skills were included. Virtually all teacher professional development programs emphasize teacher change in skills and teaching practices so that an evaluation might investigate whether there have indeed been shifts in teacher attitudes, understandings, skills, and behaviors as a function of their participation in the professional development.

Shifts in attitudes and understandings can to some extent be evaluated through self-reports from participants and relevant stakeholders, including school leaders, parents, and students. Teachers and others can also report changes in skills such as enhanced teaching and instructional activities in the classroom. For our evaluation, the value of teacher self-reports was related primarily to professional outcomes teachers perceived as relevant to their role and what they do in classrooms rather than satisfaction with the professional development program.

At another level, evaluation should involve evidence of actual teacher behavior change in the classroom associated with participation in professional development, as new skills and understandings are reflected in the teaching and learning process. Interviews and surveys can solicit teachers' self-reports of changes in their practice, but direct evidence of teacher change requires classroom observations in the context of a quasi-experimental research design to investigate differences as a function of participation in the professional development program. Teacher professional development may also have an impact on school-wide policy and classroom structures which affect students, such as grouping and 'tracking' practices that assign students to low-, middle-, or high-achievement groups for instruction.

By addressing multiple levels and factors expected to be influenced by Te Kotahitanga, the evaluation findings reported throughout this book build on and add to existing knowledge about effective teacher professional development and its evaluation. Guskey and Yoon (2009) highlight the results of a review of more than 1,300 relevant citations that revealed only nine studies meeting accepted methodological standards to attribute changes in student achievement to teacher professional development (see also Yoon et al., 2007)—none of which addresses either culturally responsive pedagogies or secondary level teacher professional development. In contrast to the majority of the literature on teacher professional development, we utilized established approaches to measuring and evaluating the effectiveness and impact of teacher professional development. These included incorporating a quasi-experimental design to examine student outcomes as a function of the program. Thus, the research reported in this book adds substantively to what is a small empirical base in an otherwise relatively large published literature.

The evaluation research questions

A comprehensive evaluation could be expected to address all of the outcomes summarized in the previous section. To do this, the approach being evaluated must be clearly described in a replicable manner and assurances given that the model has been implemented with integrity. Chapter 3 provides details regarding the Te Kotahitanga teacher professional development model and process, including its theoretical base, content, and quality monitoring processes consistent with best practices (Timperley, Wilson, Barrar, & Fung, 2007). This chapter describes the evaluation methodology, data collection processes, and analytic approaches used to examine the relationship between Te Kotahitanga and the multiple outcomes targeted by this professional development project.

The actual research questions framing the evaluation were prescribed by the New Zealand Ministry of Education, including the overarching question *How well and in what ways does Te Kotahitanga work towards the goal of improving Māori student achievement?* and a list of specific sub-questions:

- What is the quality of the overall design, content and implementation of Te Kotahitanga?
- How valuable are the outcomes for the teachers who participate— what new knowledge, understandings and skills do they develop, and how valuable are these learnings?
- How valuable are the outcomes for Māori students, and what is the impact on other classmates/peers?
- How valuable are the outcomes for family/whānau?
- How beneficial (or detrimental) are the effects of Te Kotahitanga on school culture (covering any changes in formal systems and policies; informal practices, or "the way we do things around here"; and underlying beliefs, values, assumptions and attitudes)?
- What are the enablers and barriers for getting Te Kotahitanga to work most effectively?
- To what extent is Te Kotahitanga likely to work effectively in other settings and contexts? How sustainable is the initiative likely to be when ministry investment of resources is scaled back?
- What are the most critical factors in improving teacher efficacy?

Method

To address these evaluation questions, the evaluation was mixed-methods, involving both quantitative and qualitative analyses of multiple data sources that informed one another and allowed triangulation of emerging findings (Creswell,

2009; see Meyer et al., 2010, for the full evaluation report). Evidence regarding the model and associated principles and practices was gathered directly by the research team from 22 of the secondary schools during site visits to schools participating in the first two waves of the Te Kotahitanga program, 12 schools starting in 2003 and 10 schools (out of a total of 21) starting in 2006. Purposive sampling was used to identify samples for data collection (Kline, 2009; McMillan, 1996; Shadish, Cook, & Campbell, 2001).

The data included stakeholder perspectives about the design of Te Kotahitanga, its implementation as teacher professional development, effects on students, effects on others (teachers, family, other school personnel, etc.), impact on school policy, and planning for sustainability beyond additional funding provided by the government and expert assistance provided by the Waikato research team. Interviews, observations of co-construction meetings, and observations of follow-up professional development sessions with teachers were done by the research team during site visits to the 22 schools in 2008. We also carried out a large number of systematic in vivo classroom observations at those program schools and, in 2009, at comparison schools prior to their involvement in program activities. The classroom observations were analyzed quantitatively and qualitatively, particularly for evidence of implementation of the Effective Teaching Profile (ETP) by teachers in different schools and curriculum areas. We interviewed teachers, principals, deputy principals, heads of departments, deans, lead facilitators, other program facilitators, family members, chairpersons of boards of trustees, and the students themselves. These hundreds of interviews with participants were analyzed qualitatively for key themes emerging for the different research questions. We also reviewed school and Ministry reports and other documents about Te Kotahitanga at all 32 schools in order to examine the integrity of implementation, changes to school policy as a function of the project, and the extent to which planning for sustainability was evident.

To investigate student outcomes associated with Te Kotahitanga implementation, multiple data sources were examined encompassing three broad categories: student achievement, student behavior, and students' attitudes about their learning. Sources of information on students' attitudes about their learning included interviews with school personnel and whānau/family as well as what the students had to say about their learning, about the project, and about being Māori in schools. To investigate Māori student perspectives on Te Kotahitanga and on being Māori in their schools, we interviewed focus groups of Māori students from Years 10 to 13. We reviewed available data for student social and educational outcomes in Years 9–10 for immediate effects of Te Kotahitanga, including information about student attendance, retention, percentage representation in different ability bands for core subjects, percentage representation in the school's disciplinary statistics, and preliminary achievement assessments carried out by the schools. Sources of evidence on achievement and behavior included formal assessment information as well as school reports and interviews with various constituent groups. Formal achievement results sourced by our project included Year 11–13 National Certificate of Educational Achievement (NCEA) achievement data for the original 12 schools, where program participation had begun in 2003, allowing sufficient time to investigate long term impact on student achievement. A quasi-experimental design was utilized to investigate secondary student achievement outcomes for students at Te Kotahitanga schools compared with a matched sample of non-participating schools, with the data for these analyses sourced directly from official records in national student databases.

The bicultural evaluation approach

Given the evaluation focus on teaching and learning for Māori students in mainstream schools, the evaluation reflected bicultural principles and the research team included cultural as well as methodological expertise. Seven key points were pertinent:

1. The cultural composition of our team included Māori and non-Māori members both within the core evaluation research team as well as being represented by additional international experts experienced in cultural pedagogies and independent Māori researchers contracted in the regions of the schools participating in the project;
2. Three of the six Māori research team members were involved only in the data collection on site in schools, whereas the three core Māori research evaluation team members took part in every aspect of the evaluation;
3. The research team affirmed Māori cultural protocols at every opportunity during school visits such as powhiri (formal greeting ceremony) and less formal elements of mihimihi (an introduction), hongi (pressing noses together in greeting) and me te hariru (shaking hands), waiata (Māori song), and karakia (form of prayer);

4. Whānau group meetings were informal, not time-constrained, and affirmed cultural protocols including whakatau (informal greeting ceremony), karakia, sharing of kai (food), and poroporoaki (farewell). Meetings with students were more formal, time-constrained, and included Māori cultural elements. These meetings were led by a Māori researcher. Consistent with cultural concepts regarding intellectual property, we checked our data with whānau, students and others (more detail on data checking is provided later in this chapter);

5. On some occasions, Māori professionals and whānau members felt more comfortable commenting in Māori, and our research team was prepared to reciprocate;

6. The mixed method approach of quantitative and qualitative research was generally welcomed by diverse participants from different perspectives; and

7. We worked with an external national evaluation advisory group that included persons with Māori knowledge, expertise and experience. This group provided further input and fresh eyes in reviewing key aspects of the evaluation plan and findings from different stakeholder and bicultural perspectives.

Schools participating in Te Kotahitanga

One issue that is relevant to any evaluation is the extent to which participants (schools, teachers, students, etc.) are representative of the population that is the intended target for the initiative. There are approximately 330 secondary schools in New Zealand, and the Ministry of Education selected the first 12 project schools (referred to as Phase 3) that began in 2003 based on participation in one of the schooling improvement programs that were already in place and thus provided the funding source for Te Kotahitanga activities. Selection of the second wave of project schools that began in 2006 (referred to as Phase 4) was done collaboratively by the Waikato research team and the Ministry of Education (MOE). This selection started with an advertisement in the national Gazette calling for expressions of interest from schools that required information regarding school staff, board of trustees and principal support; indication that the school's student management system could accommodate the project's needs for data; and other criteria. More than 50 schools responded, and a joint selection panel comprising project leaders along with MOE personnel then identified 21 schools invited for Phase 4 based on both the percentage of Māori students on the roll (generally higher than 20%) and geographic region (to allow the project to extend beyond the Waikato and Auckland regions where school rolls showed the highest proportion of Māori students). These selection criteria and processes allow that the school leadership at the 33 participating schools could be regarded as a biased sample, given that the principal and board of trustees had voluntarily sought external support to enhance Māori student achievement. In addition, these schools are among those in the country—almost exclusively on the North Island—with the highest numbers and proportion of Māori students, and the evaluation results cannot be generalized to other schools and regions where these factors are quite different (e.g., schools in which only a small percentage of the students are Māori and South Island schools generally).

The timeframe for school participation in the project is particularly relevant to any evaluation of long-term student achievement outcomes. Table 4.1 indicates the timeframe for implementation of Te Kotahitanga in the two sets of project schools. The first group of 12 Phase 3 schools began participation late 2003, hence 2004 was the first full year of participation and teacher training. A second group of 21 Phase 4 schools began late 2006 with initial program preparation and the teaching staff divided into three cohorts for the training years 2007, 2008, and 2009. As summarized in Table 4.1, training years are those in which cohorts of teachers are using the Te Kotahitanga model and participating in professional development activities for the first time. The years designated as full implementation for schools signify that all teachers participating in Te Kotahitanga have been trained in the model, thus all students in Years 9–10 are being exposed to Te Kotahitanga trained teachers. Year 9 students in Phase 3 schools in 2006—the first year of full implementation—will not be in the Year 11–13 student cohort until 2008–2010, and Year 9 students in Phase 4 schools in 2010—the first year of full implementation—will not be in the Year 11–13 student cohort until 2012–2014.

Full implementation of a program initiative is an important prerequisite for any evaluation of effects on student outcomes. In New Zealand, Year 9–10 secondary school students are enrolled in different subjects across the curriculum so that, on any given day, a student will be exposed to 5–6 different teachers. During the "training years", some teachers will have been trained in Te Kotahitanga and others not. Of course, even in the "full implementation" years, students will be exposed to a small number of teachers new to the program or who have chosen not to participate. This makes it difficult to quantify

Table 4.1 Implementation timeframes for Te Kotahitanga across the
two sets of participating schools

Project Year	Phase 3 Schools (N = 12)	Phase 4 Schools (N = 21)
1st Year	2004 (years 9–10) *Training Year*	2007 (years 9–10) *Training Year*
2nd Year	2005 (years 9–11) *Training Year*	2008 (years 9–11) *Training Year*
3rd Year	2006 (years 9–12) *Full Implementation*	2009 (years 9–12) *Training Year*
4th Year	2007 (years 9–13) *Full Implementation*	2010 (years 9–13) *Full Implementation*

student exposure to the Te Kotahitanga model and probably impossible to evaluate the quality of that exposure. These are the kinds of complications that make it challenging to track student outcomes as a function of teacher professional development initiatives and which must be kept in mind in reading subsequent chapters of this book.

Sample selection: Schools and participants

Participation in the evaluation overall was not voluntary to schools receiving support from the Ministry of Education and from the Waikato research team but was expected as part of the condition of funding the school received for the program. Thus, site visits to schools early in 2008 included all 12 schools that had begun participation in Te Kotahitanga in 2003. Resources did not permit replication of the intensive data collection procedures used for these 12 Phase 3 schools at all 21 Phase 4 schools, hence we elected to replicate these data collection procedures in a smaller, non-biased sample of 10 of the Phase 4 schools (approximately half). School selection was not biased with respect to factors considered likely to influence results (e.g., one school had a major school review scheduled during the week targeted for our visit, so we selected an alternative school). In 2009, the comparison sample of 10 schools was also identified from 17 new secondary schools selected for program participation in Phase 5, hence representing 'baseline' comparison data from schools that had committed to participation but had not yet actually begun program activities. Participation by these comparison schools was voluntary as this was not (yet) a condition of program participation that had not yet been initiated; two schools declined participation and alternate schools were identified.

For individual participation in the interviews and observations, participants were recruited by the school's program facilitation team working in concert with the principal. However, individual participation in these interviews
and/or observations was voluntary and accompanied by signed informed consent as required by our ethical review procedures. Participants seemed overwhelmingly enthusiastic about participation, and no one suggested there was
any undue pressure or coercion to participate from anyone at their school. The
large numbers of observations and interviews provide multiple replications for
data collection enhancing the external validity of findings (Kline, 2009). The
validity of data from naturalistic observations and independent interviews is
also supported by low-inference data collection procedures used by the evaluation project and participant familiarity with similar processes such as the
facilitator observations conducted each term (Cozby, 2009; Huck & Cormier,
1996; McMillan, 1996).

To establish a quasi-experimental design for student achievement outcome comparisons in the final years of secondary school—when assessment
grades are recorded formally in official student records—we identified a sample
of 12 "like" schools matched school-by-school with the original Phase 3 Te
Kotahitanga schools as closely as possible using the following criteria:

1. North Island state schools: As Te Kotahitanga was implemented only
    on the North Island and included only public secondary schools, the
    12 schools selected as comparison schools are also North Island and of
    a similar type (state schools, either coed or single-sex);
2. Socio-economic: Schools were matched within one decile level,
    which provides an estimate of the relative wealth of the school's sur-
    rounding community of students' families ranging from a low of 1 to
    a high of 10;
3. Percentage of Māori students at the school in 2004: The 12 Te
    Kotahitanga and 12 comparison schools had an identical mean aver-
    age of 41.4%, with no match showing more than a 20% difference;
4. Percentage of Māori students leaving school with at least a Year 12
    qualification in 2004: Across schools, the two samples showed a mean
    average difference of only 1.5%, with no match showing more than a
    11% difference;
5. Geographic location/region and school size: Following application of the
    above criteria, comparison matches were then selected based on geo-
    graphical region (e.g., both rural, small town, urban) and school size.

Table 4.2 Percentage of Māori students on the total school rolls for Te Kotahitanga and matched comparison schools, 2004–2009

	12 Te Kōtahitanga schools				12 comparison schools			
	Mean	Median	SD	SE mean	Mean	Median	SD	SE mean
2004	41.1	41.3	19.9	5.8	41.4	40.4	19.6	5.7
2005	41.8	42.7	18.8	5.4	42.6	41.2	20.0	5.8
2006	41.9	44.1	19.1	5.5	42.5	41.0	20.5	5.9
2007	42.1	45.4	19.2	5.6	43.4	41.1	21.0	6.1
2008	41.3	36.5	20.8	6.0	43.1	39.6	20.3	5.9
2009	44.0	45.3	19.5	5.6	44.3	41.4	21.3	6.1

Table 4.2 shows the Māori percentage of the school roll for each year from 2004 to 2009 for the 24 schools. While the total student roll was larger at the Te Kotahitanga schools (4,628 compared to 3,816), these samples are sufficiently large and the standard deviations comparable across the two groups so that this numerical difference should not affect the results.

Classroom observations

Classroom observations were a critical part of the evaluation in order to gather evidence regarding the implementation of culturally responsive pedagogies by trained teachers, since Māori student experiences in mainstream classrooms and schools are the primary focus of Te Kotahitanga. Classroom teaching and learning activities are the authentic measure of shifts in teachers' view of students away from deficit- to strengths-based perspectives and the transformation of classroom instruction from transmission models to more discursive, interactive models building on student culture, experiences and understandings. We observed proportionate percentages of both male and female teachers of diverse ethnicities including Māori and non-Māori, a range of subjects across Years 9–10, different levels of teaching experience, and at different ages. With the exception of a very small number of double class periods, virtually all our observations covered a full class period ranging from 45–60 minutes depending on the individual schools' daily schedule.

Of the 204 observations in March–April 2008 at the 12 Phase 3 schools, we observed a minimum of 5 lessons at the smallest school to a maximum of

34 at the largest school. The largest number of observations (nearly 100 of the total) occurred in core subjects such as English, mathematics, and science, and the smallest number occurred in elective subjects (e.g., Japanese, Māori, dance, health). Of 132 classroom observations in October 2008 at 10 Phase 4 schools, we observed a minimum of 5 lessons at the smallest schools to a maximum of 29 at two of the largest schools. Approximately 60% of these observations occurred in the core subjects of English, mathematics, science, and social studies, and the smallest number occurred in elective subjects (e.g., Japanese, Māori, technology, drama). Of these 336 observations, we dropped 18 that were invalid for various reasons (e.g., teacher not participating in the professional development program, outdoor class rained out, class time being used for something other than instruction), leaving us with 318 observations to analyze across the two sets of schools.

At the 10 comparison Phase 5 schools, 98 classroom observations in four core subjects were conducted (English, science, mathematics, social studies). The data from these schools also provide Te Kotahitanga with baseline, pre-intervention data that can be used for comparisons post-intervention.

The classroom observation data sheet developed by core project personnel included the following:

- Basic demographic information (school, teacher, subject, ethnicity, year level, date, etc.)
- Room environment (physical description of the classroom, seating, teacher positioning, cultural visuals in the room, etc.)
- Lesson narrative (running record for the first and final five minutes of the lesson, how the teacher greeted students, mention of expectations, stating learning outcomes, references to Māori culture/names, etc.)
- Māori curriculum content (use of Māori intellectual knowledge, etc.)
- Effective Teaching Profile (ETP) (examples or missed opportunities for each of the 6 major dimensions: Manākitanga (caring for students as culturally located individuals); Mana motuhake (high expectations for learning); Whakapiringatanga (managing the classroom for learning); Wānanga (discursive teaching practices and student-student learning interactions); Ako (range of strategies to facilitate learning); and Kotahitanga (promote, monitor and reflect on learning outcomes with students)

- Teaching and learning types (10-minute interval recording of how instruction was organized, including teacher presentations with different types of questions, group work, individual seatwork, project activities, student-led presentations, and non-academic and transition times)

Lessons were evaluated for implementation of the ETP based on the records for each lesson observed. High Implementation and Low Implementation (including missed opportunities) were coded as specified below, and "Implementation" was coded for observations that were neither High nor Low:

High Implementation

- Some evidence of at least 5 of the 6 ETP dimensions
- Strong evidence for at least 2 ETP dimensions
- Must include explicit cultural references
- Must reference learning outcomes/objectives/aims
- Evidence of positive teacher-student relationships
- Positive classroom management supporting learning

Low Implementation

- No evidence of any of the ETP dimensions observed
- Alternatively, weak examples or missed opportunities
- Misconceptions or inaccuracies/wrong message
- Mismanagement of the classroom disrupting learning

These three categories had been developed through initial review of a subsample of the observations. Consensus was reached on coding criteria, and different researcher pairs were assigned to code each observation; no one coded lessons he/she had observed and each researcher coder was paired with one another for at least some coding. For disagreements across the two independent coders, 3–4 researchers reached consensus through discussion. Results were summarized by subjects across schools and by school across subjects, identifying exemplars at different implementation levels (see also Savage et al., 2011).

Interviews

Table 4.3 provides an overall summary of interviews conducted during the site visits to the 22 program schools. Individual interviews were conducted in

Table 4.3 Summary of Interview Data

Participants	Number	Sample Interview Topics	Interview Type
Teachers	150	• Perceived effects on agency and expectations for Māori student achievement • Impact on practice including culturally responsive pedagogies • Attitudes towards different components of program • Reports of impact on Māori student outcomes and sources of evidence • Opinions regarding the ETP versus "good teaching" generally	• Individual • Focus group
School Leaders • Principals • Deputy Principals	 20 19	• School policy and practices towards attainment of Te Kotahitanga program goals • Plans and actions for sustainability • School leaders' approaches to reflecting Te Kotahitanga principles in their role	• Individual
Middle Managers • Deans • Heads of Department	 22 19	• Use of evidence by the school to support efforts to enhance Māori student achievement • Perceived value of program outcomes for Māori students, all students, and school personnel • Feedback from teachers, parents, etc., about the program • Opinions about quality of the program, its different components, and implementation at the school	• Individual or focus groups of 2–3
Program Facilitators • Lead Facilitators • Facilitator Team Member	 22 32	• Opinions about the impact of the program on teachers and students, and sources of evidence for those opinions • Perceptions regarding the quality of program components at their school • Beliefs regarding valuable outcomes for students and teachers • What they regard as enablers and barriers to implementation and program effectiveness • What additional training and/or support might be helpful and contribute to sustainability	• Individual • Individual or focus groups

(continued)

Table 4.3 Summary of Interview Data (*continued*)

Participants	Number	Sample Interview Topics	Interview Type
Māori students Years 10–13	214	• Meaning of Te Kotahitanga to Māori students • How students feel about school and their learning • In what ways they are able, or not able, to "learn as Māori" • Whether being Māori is the same or different in school versus outside school • How their cultural identity is, or is not, affirmed at school	• Focus groups
Chairpersons of School Boards of Trustees	15	• Why and how the Board supports Te Kotahitanga, at initial adoption, currently, and in the future • Perceived impact of the program on the school (positive and negative) • Impressions about program quality and data sources for information • Enablers and barriers for sustainability	• Individual
Māori family members (whānau)	19 groups*	• Meaning of Te Kotahitanga to Māori families and students • Perceived impact of program on their child's achievement and other behaviours (e.g., attendance, enjoyment of school) • Perceived changes in how school personnel (teachers, others) approach students and families	• Focus groups

* These groups ranged from 2–3 participants to more than 15 participants, sometimes coming and going throughout the session.

a private space involving only the interviewee and the researcher conducting the interview; individual interviews were digitally recorded using high-quality, small digital recorders generally positioned on a table or chair close to both persons. Interview participants were provided the full list of questions prior to or at the time of the interview, and a set of indicative questions was made available for the school to share with interviewees in advance of the interviews. Most interviewees had not seen the questions prior to the interview but indicated they had knowledge of the focus of the evaluation; if they had not already signed consent, they did so at the time of the interview.

Focus group interviews were also held in a location separate from other activities; these were conducted by two researchers using note-taking rather than digital recording. Following introductions, one researcher served as facilitator to introduce the questions and would begin by reading out all the 4–5 focus group questions to the group then returning to the questions one at a time to allow for group responses. This group facilitator gave full attention to group responses, including making decisions along the way regarding the need for probe questions or examples for clarification. The second researcher assumed a listening role and was responsible for taking detailed notes to record virtually all verbal responses in writing. Immediately after the group indicated that they had made all comments considered relevant to each question or issue, the note-taker read out the recorded responses to the group to allow for additions and edits and to check for accuracy. Changes and additions were then made at that time according to input from the group. This process encourages focus groups to take an active role in listening to input from everyone in the group (one at a time rather than speaking all at once) and ensures that all voices are heard rather than allowing domination by a one or a few members. Just as important, it has an advantage over digital recording followed by transcription in providing immediate member-checking of the validity and reliability of the information recorded by the researcher/s, and participants commented favorably on the process and the accuracy of our notes.

Pairings of researchers conducting the focus groups were influenced by scheduling logistics. An additional consideration for all Māori student and whānau focus groups was to ensure that they were led by a Māori facilitator who was fluent in Māori and knowledgeable regarding Māori cultural protocols. Focus group meetings with families followed marae informal meeting protocols and generally began with mihimihi, and the research team provided for a light supper and drinks so a karakia was also said. Focus group interviews with groups of students and teachers were up to an hour long; those with family members extended to as much as two hours.

Interviews were recorded digitally, and typed Word transcripts were coded by experienced coders using NVivo. The researchers reviewed printed transcripts and met to review possible codes towards identifying themes in the interview data, based on their experiences having carried out the interviews. Codes were identified by two core researchers based on a sub-sample of complete interview transcriptions to identify possible nodes and words for coding using NVivo, and the full set of codes was discussed further with the international consultant and an additional researcher team member prior to coding all data. Once the data were coded, themes were identified from the data by those same team members and salient quotes identified to illustrate the themes. Following initial coding using NVivo of a sample of teacher interviews, however, it was decided to analyze the full set of teacher interviews manually with researcher pairs independently reviewing complete transcripts and raising proposed themes for further discussion across the research team.

Evidence on student outcomes

There were limitations resulting from the nature of the evaluation design, the start date for the evaluation, and various practical constraints affecting the extent to which changes in student achievement and achievement-related outcomes could be attributed to Te Kotahitanga. The schools' contractual agreements with the Ministry of Education did not require them to administer measures of achievement in the different subject areas, nor were we able as part of the evaluation to administer such achievement measures directly in project schools. The schools did not have particular expertise in administration, scoring, and interpreting achievement measures in Years 9–10, nor are agreed measures available that have validity and can be scored and interpreted reliably. Some schools had used a standardized test of numeracy and literacy with students, but not all schools had done so.

Without specific information regarding the variation and discrepancies in the availability of assessment results, our independent evaluation team judged that the representativeness of these data could not be established. In addition, even if all schools had administered tests in numeracy and literacy, these domains did not cover subjects taught directly by teachers in the program. New Zealand schools do not record formal grades for student work until Years 11 to 13 (the final three years of high school) hence the absence of formal grades in Year 9–10 subjects was beyond either the program or evaluation teams' control.

Nevertheless, the availability of the NCEA national database for all students and all schools at the senior secondary school level did provide opportunity to investigate longer term student achievement. At the Phase 3 schools that began the professional development program in 2003, sufficient time had passed for students taught by teachers participating in the Te Kotahitanga program to reach the senior secondary school where formal achievement results are recorded for the National Certificate of Educational Achievement (NCEA) and thus available for comparative analysis. Thus, as reported in Chapter 7, we examined various NCEA achievement data across time for the 12 Phase 3 Te Kotahitanga schools in comparison to students whose teachers working with equivalent student samples including Māori students at mainstream schools not participating in Te Kotahitanga. To evaluate the impact of Te Kotahitanga on these student achievement outcomes, we compared student outcomes at schools where teachers were participating in the program with those at similar, non-participating schools across the same timeframe. Longitudinal data on student achievement in the senior secondary school (Years 11–13) for students whose Year 9–10 teachers had participated in Te Kotahitanga were sourced directly from official records in national student databases. The vast majority of senior high school subjects are taught by the very same teachers working with Year 9–10 students, who might thus be expected to transfer their new skills in culturally responsive pedagogies across into senior subjects. Of course, whether or not they do so is unknown.

Our evaluation team has recommended to government that, in future, such initiatives should require schools to administer an agreed achievement measure alongside initiatives intended to enhance student achievement. We also consider it important to determine the extent to which teachers trained in new and enhanced pedagogies are able to transfer mastery to teaching at other levels and in other subjects. For now, this issue remains unanswered.

Linking Teacher Professional Development to Student Outcomes

The comprehensive Te Kotahitanga evaluation encompassed multiple data sources, including systematic observation of more than 400 secondary classrooms across the curriculum at program and comparison schools; individual and focus group interviews with approximately 300 educators, more than 200 students, and dozens of family members; and analyses of school and national databases recording student achievement, behavior, and attitudes about their learning. As is reported throughout this book, these data revealed multiple outcomes that can be associated with participation in Te Kotahitanga. Ultimately, the purpose of teacher professional development towards improving classroom instruction is not just teacher behavior change, but also the enhancement of student achievement. Effective teacher professional development is designed to change teaching practices as an important pathway towards improving student learning outcomes (Darling-Hammond & McLaughlin, 1995; Little, 1993). What is the evidence that teacher professional development will have a positive impact on student achievement?

In the introduction to this chapter, several steps were described that require documentation for teacher professional development that can lead to changes in student achievement. First, the professional development must have the potential to effect the intended changes in teacher knowledge, skills, and understandings. There are agreed criteria for quality teacher professional development incorporating issues such as its theoretical base, content quality, content validity, and the educational process for effective adult and professional learning (Garet et al., 2001; Wilson & Berne, 1999). Next, teachers must apply what they have learned to their classroom teaching and instructional practices. Teachers can express satisfaction with what they have learned and even be able to talk about these new understandings in detail, but the crucial issue is whether they change what happens in the classroom. Enhanced teacher knowledge and skills can also be related to improvements in classroom climate that may in turn be associated with enhanced student attendance, retention, and engagement in learning activities. These changes are desirable and important, but stakeholders also expect improvement in student achievement outcomes. The challenge is that the relationship between a teacher professional development program and student achievement is complex and dependent on documentation of intervening changes in teacher behavior. Hence, missing or weak links will seriously limit the impact on student outcomes (Yoon et al., 2007).

Thus it may not be surprising that there are so few empirical studies demonstrating a direct relationship between teacher professional development and student achievement. The vast majority of the published literature in this area is not empirical research reporting impact on students but instead comprises theoretical papers, opinion pieces, commentaries, unpublished conference papers, and qualitative studies such as interviews with teachers about their satisfaction or beliefs rather than systematic analyses of student achievement change as a function of teacher professional development. Nor is there strong evidence based on observational data showing changes in teaching practice and learning activities in classrooms as a function of teacher professional development. In their review of more than 1,300 studies purporting to investigate the effects of teacher professional development on student achievement, Yoon et al. (2007) found only a handful that met minimal evidence standards criteria to affirm a relationship between these two factors. While the size of the database overall is disappointing, the nine studies that did meet evidence standards established by the What Works Clearinghouse supported a moderate effect on student achievement as a function of teacher professional development.

Guskey and Yoon (2009) and Yoon et al. (2007) discuss the methodological issues that must be considered for valid evidence that teacher professional development has an impact on students. A study comparing outcomes for two groups—one receiving the teacher professional development intervention and the second group that did not—is one approach to evaluating the impact of teacher professional development. For a comparison study to be valid, the baseline equivalence of the intervention and comparison groups (schools, teachers, and students) must be supported with respect to key variables that might be expected to influence the outcome. So, for example, to evaluate an intervention designed to enhance teacher skills in culturally responsive pedagogies, the intervention and comparison groups should be similar or equivalent on factors such as baseline cultural diversity of the schools; expertise and experience of the teachers; financial resources; other ongoing interventions; and commitment to enhance student achievement. True experimental designs are not feasible in the absence of control over the assignment of schools and others to intervention and control groups. Quasi-experimental design variations can assign schools and participants to intervention and control groups by randomly identifying those who receive the intervention first, then relegating others to a "waitlist control" group that receives the intervention at a later date. This would allow the control group waiting for the intervention to be compared to the group receiving the intervention.

A quasi-experimental design requires that experimental and comparison groups are matched on key variables that could be related to the intervention focus and affect the outcome. In this design, the 'control' group is not necessarily waiting for the intervention but is shown to be equivalent to the intervention group. Even quasi-experimental designs can be challenging for applied research in schools with respect to identifying and measuring the key factors considered essential to affirming equivalence between groups. We had no control over the selection of the intervention schools, a process that had occurred several years prior to the evaluation. Hence, we utilized comparisons across schools matched for key demographic factors relevant to the longer term impact of teacher professional development on student achievement in secondary school. As mentioned earlier in this chapter, all 9 of the studies that Yoon et al. (2007) identified as meeting minimal evidence criteria were at elementary school level. To date, the New Zealand Te Kotahitanga evaluation research appears to be the only research at secondary level evaluating the relationship between teacher professional development and student outcomes.

· 5 ·

PROFESSIONAL DEVELOPMENT FROM TEACHER AND FACILITATOR PERSPECTIVES

Anne Hynds, Victoria University
Christine E. Sleeter, California State University Monterey Bay

As explained in Chapter 3, the Te Kotahitanga professional development program was designed to empower secondary school teachers to improve achievement of Māori students by developing a cultural pedagogy of relations within classrooms. The professional development model is an iterative research and development model that links culturally relevant/relationship-based classroom pedagogy with a site-based process for working with teachers in the classroom, using the Effective Teaching Profile as a basis.

Te Kotahitanga presents a partnership learning challenge to mainstream secondary schools: a bi-cultural commitment to professional learning activities underpinned by Kaupapa Māori metaphors such as ako (reciprocal teaching and learning), tino rangatiratanga (self-determination) and whakawhanaungatanga (building relationships). The challenge is significant because it calls for a repositioning of Māori worldviews and knowledge systems within schooling institutions dominated by Pākehātanga (socialization into the worldview of New Zealand Europeans) (Penetito, 2010). Unequal power relationships within mainstream schooling systems have resulted in a lack of responsiveness and inclusiveness of the education system towards Māori. As Penetito (2001) has argued, "The New Zealand education system has always operated as though all its clients were either Pākehā or wanted to become Pākehā; Māori had much to learn from Pākehā but Pākehā had little to learn from Māori" (p. 18). Consequently, partnership work involving Māori and their knowledge must be conducted in culturally appropriate ways and promote new forms of consciousness and transformative action (Bishop & Glynn, 1999).

The Te Kotahitanga program requires shared responsibility and collective agency if improvements are to be made and sustained across schools. Effective partnerships, underpinned by learning conversations between Māori and non-Māori school community members (teachers, facilitators, students, and whānau, parents, caregivers) are therefore critical to the success of Te Kotahitanga. According to Timperley and Robinson (2002) there are different dimensions underpinning effective partnership work in schools, particularly within the context of teachers' professional learning and ongoing school reform. Partnerships are often formed for specific aims, such as improving classroom practice and student learning outcomes. Two specific dimensions which impact on the effectiveness of teacher partnership activities include tasks and relationships. The ways relationships develop often determine the success of achieving the task. Integrating both the relationship and task dimensions effectively requires partners to work together and learn from one another. Effective partnerships ensure that shared responsibility to achieve stated goals are underpinned by mutual values of trust and respect, which in turn encourage differing beliefs and values to be brought to the work.

Māori and non-Māori teachers and facilitators bring their own personal histories, unique identities and culturally mediated practices into the context of partnership work (Hynds, 2007). Teacher identities encompass multiple identity markers that intersect with individual, cultural and professional values, beliefs and assumptions about what constitutes 'good teaching' and improved student outcomes. Making such assumptions about teaching and learning visible across classrooms is essential if teachers are to work with others and learn to make lessons more relevant and motivating for culturally diverse groups of learners. It is the diversity of ideas that present great potential and opportunity for new learning and growth. However, partnership work is often undermined when shared tasks are dominated by one partner's beliefs and biases (Timperley & Robinson, 2002). Consequently, commitment to shared reflection, dialogue and continued inquiry related to both task and relationship dimensions is essential if partners are to learn to improve practice together (Timperley & Robinson, 2002). Such work can be challenging, particularly within traditional secondary school systems with established hierarchies and power structures (Hynds, 2007).

In this chapter, we examine how school staff experienced the professional development model, giving specific attention to the development and enactment of partnership relationships between teachers and facilitators, and between Māori and non-Māori, since these relationships form the core of the broader project of developing culturally responsive teaching through a pedagogy of relations. We draw on the following data sets: our observations of most of the elements of the professional development process, interviews with teachers about the professional development model, interviews with facilitators about the model and their work, and interviews with school administrators about their perceptions of the effectiveness of the model.

Perceptions of the Professional Development Model

We asked principals, other members of the school leadership team (deputy principals and heads of departments), teachers, and facilitators about their perceptions of the Te Kotahitanga professional development model.

All of the principals, as well as most other leaders we interviewed, enthusiastically emphasised its value, using phrases such as "by far the most effective professional development I've ever seen," "an outstanding process," and "it should be in every school throughout the country." They saw it as very well conceptualised, and as offering far more substance than what is usually the case in professional development; several expressed appreciation for its focus on improving what happens in the classroom. One principal commented that, "It's made me think along different lines in terms of the way in which we do professional development. [It's] made me observe teaching practice and learning in a slightly different way than I would have done before I became involved with Te Kotahitanga." School leaders also saw the model as changing how teachers talk about students. As one put it:

> To be brutally honest, what I don't hear anymore—whether it was here or at other schools—I do not hear "those Māori kids" I do not hear that conversation. And for too long, staffrooms have been full of dissenters. "Oh, I can't teach them." You know what I'm saying? So those conversations have almost dried up. And that may be due to a number of factors, maybe because there was nobody else listening anymore. That number of dissenters has almost disappeared. So has it changed staff behavior? Absolutely!

Teachers' comments about the model were also overwhelmingly positive. We repeatedly heard comments such as, "It's so good you want more," and "It's been the best professional development for me, really helped me to reflect on my teaching and on what I can do it help the kids learning . . . so it's all good." One theme in their comments was their valuing the opportunity to reflect on their practice that the program prompted. The phrase "reflection on your own practice" was heard several times, and was supported by how facilitators discussed their work with teachers:

> We question them, get them to self assess. [With] self reflecting, it's not that we're telling them you have to do this, or you should be doing this. They're reflecting on their own practice and they have to see I could do this. That doesn't take that much more to do, I could do that—and I could see how this could then fit the kids and make my life easier.

Several teachers appreciated learning a different way of teaching. As one pointed out, she had "been trained as a teacher who teaches with desks placed in rows, and very much transmissive"; it had not occurred to her that there was a different approach to teaching. Several teachers said that they valued the program's focus on Māori culture, its ability to help them understand their Māori students better, and the opportunity to learn cultural concepts such as mana (personal prestige and character), wairua (spirit or soul), and manākitanga (care and hospitality for others). For some international teachers, this was their first sustained opportunity to learn about Māori culture.

The few negative teacher comments focused on four concerns. First, several teachers were put off by what they saw as its focus on Māori students to exclusion of other groups; as one put it, "If all kids are important, why do we just pick out the Māori kids?" Second, a few teachers disliked the idea that deficit theorising blamed teachers for low Māori student achievement, pointing out that there are other influences on student achievement besides the teacher. Third, a few teachers and facilitators commented that when participation in the program was compulsory, teachers resisted. Fourth, a few commented that the program needs to be more responsive to the needs of different subject areas.

The facilitators, as one might expect, were very positive about the model. They believed that the structure of the Te Kotahitanga professional development cycle—in-class observation and feedback, goal setting, shadow-coaching and co-construction meetings—enabled teachers to make positive changes. They talked about it from the vantage point of being both facilitators and also teachers. For example, one stated: "[It's] the best professional program I've ever been involved in, the most effective one. For me as a teacher because it forces me to look at what I'm doing and to make changes." The facilitators emphasised that the structure Te Kotahitanga provided helped teachers to set goals and reflect on their work, giving them the basis for making needed changes to their classroom programs. This in turn supported the notion of teachers being responsible for their class, which benefits all students. For example,

> Across the school one of our goals, and our strategic plans is to improve formative assessment. The professional development structure is very much based on Te Kotahitanga, where we have a number of facilitators, we've had ten facilitators across department groups. This involved some professional development, followed by setting some goals in our groups, group goals and individual goals and then you come back and, and share evidence of what we've been doing.

Some facilitators also emphasised the centrality to the program of embedding Māori and non-Māori partnerships within the school. As one commented, "It was Ako (reciprocal teaching and learning), right from the beginning it has been a two way thing, partnerships with all our Māori other staff in the school. There has been good support with everyone down to the Māori lady who works in the library."

Experiences with Elements of the Professional Development Model

We asked teachers and facilitators to comment on elements of the professional development model. Those elements, described in more detail in Chapter 3, include:

- *Initial hui (meeting)*. During the initial three-day hui in the marae, teachers examine the relationship between deficit theorising, pedagogy, and Māori student achievement, and learn about the process of the professional development program itself.
- *Classroom observations with feedback*. Classroom observations, carried out once per term for each teacher by a facilitator using the Te Kotahitanga Observation Tool, are followed by feedback in which the facilitator and teacher meet to discuss the lesson and recorded data.
- *Shadow-coaching sessions*. Shadow-coaching follows a similar process except that it focuses on something specific the teacher would like help with, with the facilitator acting as "guide on the side."

- **Co-construction meetings**. Small numbers of teachers who teach the same students but in different subject areas meet once every month or two to share concerns and strategies for improving Māori student achievement.

We were able to observe instances of each of these elements except the initial hui, none of which were scheduled during the time we visited the schools. In what follows, we present patterns in what we saw, followed by what we heard during interviews.

The initial hui: What we heard

When we asked teachers about the professional development model, a few talked specifically about the initial hui, although for many we interviewed, this experience was probably distant enough that they did not talk directly about it. Most comments about the hui were positive, such as "awesome," "brilliant," and "lovely." Teachers who commented on its impact mainly focused on the power of the narratives in *Culture Speaks* (Bishop & Berryman, 2006) to help them understand the point of view of the students and whānau (family), and to put words to the idea of deficit theorising. A couple of teachers also commented that the hui was a great way to begin the year and to integrate new teachers with the rest of the staff.

There were isolated criticisms of it. A couple of teachers thought the presentation of statistics (regarding Māori student achievement) was too abstract, a couple were critical of the time the hui took when they needed time for planning, and one maths teacher wanted more linkage between the ideas presented and mathematics.

Classroom observations with feedback

Classroom observations, which are jointly scheduled ahead of time, last one class period. Feedback sessions, which usually occur on the same day, follow a specific structure. First, the facilitator asks the teacher to comment on how the lesson went. Second, the facilitator and teacher review and discuss notes from the observation. Some of the notes record fairly objective data, such as records of the engagement of the specific Māori students the facilitator was focusing on, or instances in which the teacher encouraged dialogue. Other notes are more evaluative, particularly a section where teachers are rated on a scale from 1 to 5 on various dimensions of "Evidence of Relationships." Finally, feedback sessions should conclude with the facilitator and teacher reflecting together on the helpfulness of the feedback, joint problem-solving on issues raised, and identifying next steps.

What we saw

We observed 24 feedback sessions following classroom observations. Notes were too sketchy or inaudible for analysis of 4 of them, giving us 20 sessions to analyze. We classified them into three categories: (1) facilitator-dominant, (2) facilitator-dominant but including some substantive instances of joint activity, and (3) co-constructed with joint activity throughout. We used this classification in order to explore how teachers and facilitators positioned themselves in relationship to each other, since the professional development process is intended to model the reciprocal discursive relations that Te Kotahitanga works to bring about.

Six feedback sessions we observed were facilitator-dominant. In these sessions, after the teacher reflected on the lesson and the pair began to consider data in the facilitator's observation, the facilitator took over and did most of the talking and agenda-setting, and the teacher's utterances diminished considerably. For example, in one observation the facilitator talked while most of the teacher's utterances were "Mmmm" or "Yep." In another, as a teacher reflected on a problem, the facilitator, rather than responding, went onto another topic. Facilitator-dominant sessions tended to conclude with little or no reflection on the observation or on what the teacher would work on next. At the end of one of these sessions, the facilitator commented to the member of our team who was taking notes that she was aware that her feedback sessions tended to be too top-down rather than collaborative, and that she would welcome strategies to make the feedback structure more give-and-take; she did not seem to know how to shift the power dynamics.

Ten feedback sessions we observed were facilitator-dominant but included some substantive instances of joint activity. For example, in one session, the facilitator was telling the teacher how well she was doing towards reaching her goals. The teacher responded:

> That's true to an extent, but I don't think I got there. There's a lot in Michael that I'm not seeing yet. Shelly, she's come along in leaps and bounds. She overwhelms

me. Michael is quiet, the girls are so good to him, they understand his quietness. The three boys are confident and capable, but nowhere near where they could be. They sit back under the radar.

Rather than moving on to the next topic, the facilitator responded by looking at the data from the observation, which both then discussed. These ten sessions tended to conclude with more reflection that was done jointly than did the facilitator-dominant sessions. For example, toward the end of one, the facilitator asked the teacher what goal he would be working on. As he responded, the facilitator wrote his response on the feedback form. She then asked: "So, what planning will you do to achieve it?" He suggested several ideas. Then the facilitator asked, "What effect will this have on your relationships with Māori students?" He replied, "They like to achieve. If you pick them out as an individual, they don't like that, but if they are all working together, good." The facilitator responded with, "You're reflective, you're not doing the same old same old, you're trying something new. What learning experiences do you want your Māori students to have?" The teacher then discussed working to help students see that answering something wrong is better that not participating out of fear of giving a wrong answer. Although much of the facilitator's participation in this exchange was to ask questions, her questions built on the teacher's responses, prompting further reflection.

Four feedback sessions we observed were largely co-constructed with considerable joint activity. In contrast to the facilitator-dominant sessions, often the teachers talked through problems while the facilitator listened with encouragement, such as, "Mmmm," and "āe (yes)." For example:

Teacher: One of the things that I realize now is that I need to have a strategy to help the students with their spelling.

Facilitator: āe.

Teacher: And you know, instead of me going around and them asking me how to spell the word.

Facilitator: āe.
Teacher: I need to have some sort of strategy, and I might have to go to their English teacher. . .

Facilitator: Yeah, well there's [name] in our cluster, you know, she might be able to provide some insight into your questions.

In these four sessions, the teacher set the agenda for collaborative discussion as often as did the facilitator. For example, a facilitator and mathematics teacher were considering how the teacher should be rated on "Evidence of

Relationships." The teacher, who must have been thinking this over, commented, "I need to work on fractions somewhere else along the way, their understanding is not there for Year 11." The facilitator commented, "Great, you're identifying a gap." The teacher went on to reflect on a problem with lower level classes in which students talk too much and listen too little. Then he asked, "Is it alright to keep explaining the whole thing? By the third day I'm still giving a definition." The two then brainstormed, in a back and forth fashion, how the teacher might better engage the students.

What we heard

Of the various elements of the professional development model, teachers commented on and expressed most enthusiasm about the process of classroom observations followed by feedback sessions. We heard very few negative comments about this part of the program, and many very positive comments such as "awesome," "brilliant," "fantastic," and "great." Teachers appreciated the observations for various reasons. Several teachers valued the observation data on their teaching, such as which students they interacted with and which they missed. They commented that having another set of eyes in the classroom was incredibly valuable; as one teacher put it, "You can only look in one direction at a time." Teachers appreciated being able to see their progress with students over time. Several noted that once teachers have been hired and completed the first couple of years of teaching, they may never again get feedback on their practice. They valued the practical suggestions and ideas they were offered. Several mentioned that this professional development process up-skills teachers, building on what they learned in their teacher training program and adding to their teaching repertoire. One commented that over time if no adult holds them accountable, they just "switch off."

Teachers valued the support given after the observations. Several described the process of being observed, then discussing the observation, as promoting reflection on their practice. One teacher commented, for example, that the process "forces me outside my comfort zone and it was quite scary at first . . . but now I really look forward to the observation and feedback sessions." While teachers often felt nervous at the beginning of the process, less than a half-dozen teachers described the process of being observed as threatening and persistently uncomfortable. The great majority embraced it as a form of professional development with enthusiasm.

Similarly, the lead facilitators believed that teachers found the classroom observations and reflections useful. They pointed out that the cycle of in-class observation, feedback and analysis had enabled teachers to work more professionally. They saw the observation tool and feedback loop as being critical; as one put it, "It's amazing, I look what a feedback [session] does to kind of help someone look forward. A thing that happens with kids, and [teachers] get feedback. The observation tool for teachers is a huge thing." This process of a facilitator observing a teacher and then providing feedback changed the belief that teachers own their classrooms and need to defend their territories; as a facilitator put it, "People used to own their territory, don't you dare come in here and tell me to observe what I'm doing. But now [being observed] is an expectation, that is a big change and it is working as a professional with other professionals."

This professional development process, particularly the effort to establish dialogical relationships, was new to everyone. The facilitators were learning how to act as facilitators, and the teachers were learning how to engage in the process. Some facilitators commented that their role was very new and 'foreign,' and as teachers they had never experienced a similar professional development program. This lack of prior experience could impact on a facilitator's sense of confidence role: "It's quite a foreign process to me. I've never had a shadow coaching or that particular observation tool, or co-construction meetings. I've never done any of that in any school I've been at." It is likely that difficulties some facilitators experienced in attempting to establish dialogical relationships with teachers in feedback sessions was due to their newness to the process.

Shadow-coaching

The main difference between shadow-coaching and formal observations was that teachers defined the focus for shadow-coaching (such as asking higher order questions), rather than the focus being defined specifically by the Effective Teaching Profile. We were told that in several schools, shadow-coaching was used infrequently, however, because of limits on facilitators' available time. For that reason, in some schools shadow-coaching had not been put into place. As one facilitator explained, "We make it through to observations [and] feedback about individual goals, but [we're] not getting to the follow-up for everybody. The hardest part is following those teachers up as well . . . there're not enough hours in the day. I mean, I'm busy, they're busy."

What we saw

We observed three feedback sessions following shadow-coaching. Across these there was variation in facilitator practices and the extent to which shadow-coaching was a joint activity co-constructed between both parties. One session was clearly driven by the teacher, and the facilitator served as support as the teacher worked through a problem; a second was partially teacher-driven and partially facilitator-driven, and the third was completely facilitator-dominant. We had been told that shadow-coaching involved the facilitator giving the teacher input throughout the lesson rather than observing and then providing feedback afterward, but what we saw followed the observation-feedback process rather than in-class modeling and assistance.

In the teacher led session we observed, the teacher led the majority of the discussion. The teacher reiterated that her goal was to improve feedforward strategies, as well as student reflection within a particular classroom. This goal had come out of the teacher's efforts to improve higher-order thinking within the class. At this meeting, the teacher had brought examples of student work as well as other evidence of teacher feedback/feedforward strategies used with individual Māori students within the class. The facilitator listened, rephrased teacher comments and asked probing questions to prompt teacher reflection around student ownership and understanding of assessment tasks. For example, the facilitator asked; "How did you feel about the use of these . . . strategies?" The teacher replied, "Like this (teacher shares an example of student work) when they are writing by themselves, a lot come up to me with questions and I'm able to redirect them (to the assessment task) and ask why have you done this? . . . so prompting them to figure out what to do next . . . they're still looking to a degree to me for the answers . . . but that's part of growing up . . . but the strategies are really useful."

In the second observation the co-construction meeting was partially led by the teacher and partially by the facilitator. The teacher's goal was to encourage quieter Māori students to participate actively in class and group discussions. In this session both the teacher and facilitator reflected on the use of resources and new strategies being trialed by the teacher. The meeting started with the facilitator asking most of the questions and reflecting on the progress of individual students. At this stage the teacher affirmed the facilitator, commenting "Yes" and "Yup". However, after a while the teacher started to participate more, and at times led the discussion, particularly as the conversation turned towards the progress of individual students.

In the facilitator-dominant session, it appeared that the teacher was really struggling with behavior management issues and needed in-class coaching and specific practice of new pedagogies. The facilitator explained to the observer that she had been in the teacher's class every day that week. Both looked at the data on the observation sheet and in particular the student engagement data, with the facilitator doing the most of the talking. After a while the facilitator said, "Well I've talked enough, we need your observations". However rather than waiting for the teacher to respond the facilitator then got out a post-observation sheet and continued going over what was recorded on it. Later the facilitator asked, "What will it (your goal) look like in class?" The teacher responded by saying "There will be more respect for the teacher. . . . That's how I see it in my head, but when I get to class sometimes it doesn't go that way". The facilitator appeared to ignore the teacher comments and the discussion ended by both parties talking about involving students in the development of class resources.

What we heard

Teachers' remarks about shadow-coaching were more varied than they were about the formal observation and feedback sessions. In several interviews, teachers were not sure what the difference was between the two. The effectiveness of shadow-coaching from the teachers' perspective appeared to be dependent on the facilitator's knowledge of the process and/or skill in aligning the process to teachers' individual needs. For example, one teacher said:

> I like the observations, and again, I think it's some useful data on what I'm doing. Shadow coaching has been variable, as it depends on who's been observing and what they've had to offer. Sometimes it's been fantastic and they have actually sat down with me and said "here's a different way you could've done it, and here's some ideas" and I've found that really [useful], and other times they haven't really offered anything at all, and so that has varied from person to person and observation to observation.

Several facilitators also acknowledged that shadow-coaching was not working as effectively as other components of the professional development model. Some acknowledged that they lacked expertise and knowledge of its process, purpose and structure, and that they themselves had not actually done shadow-coaching yet.

Co-construction meetings

Co-construction meetings are led by the facilitator who has observed the participating teachers. The intended focus of co-construction meetings is the analysis of a teaching-learning problem shared by the teaching team, using some form of evidence of learning, then developing a group goal. At a subsequent meeting, the group analyses what they have been doing to improve their practice relative to that goal. For co-construction meetings to work as intended, teacher participants should bring evidence from both the observations as well as student achievement–related data such as attendance, disciplinary events, and so on.

What we saw

We observed three co-construction meetings. In all three, the facilitator began by stating the agenda, then laying the ground rules for discussion, which included confidentiality and the expectation that the focus be on student achievement. In all three meetings, teacher talk dominated, with teachers taking turns. Most teacher talk involved sharing anecdotes related to students they were discussing. Teachers often began by describing how a student had achieved in a test or assignment (but without bringing samples of the students' work), and the discussion moved from there into other areas of the student's work or behavior that teachers had concerns or anecdotes about. Teachers shared problems, concerns, or dilemmas they were grappling with (such a student's irregular attendance), and solutions they had tried.

What we heard

The teachers generally found co-construction meetings valuable. About one-third of the teachers commented on them, and about three-fourths of these comments were positive. Teachers said that they valued the time to reflect and to solve problems with other teachers who are working with the same students, and that usually teachers do not get time to do this. For example, one teacher explained that, "We had one co-construction meeting where it became fairly obvious that we were all struggling with the same people and the same issues"; teachers then brainstormed strategies that might engage these students better. Another teacher explained that the team developed consistency in their approach to working with students, which stopped students from trying to get away with things. Teachers in co-construction groups that worked well described the group as a "professional learning community" they found very supportive. The few teachers who did not find the co-construction meetings beneficial cited logistical or planning problems: a few were assigned to a group based on one of their classes that was not actually the one in which they needed help; a couple of teachers experienced inconsistency between the co-construction group facilitator and the facilitator who was observing them in the classroom; and a couple of teachers commented that use of a non-contact period for co-construction meetings took away from time to plan for classes.

According to the facilitators, the quality of evidence used generally in co-construction meetings or within the school to assess Māori students' progress varied, and teachers often shared anecdotal evidence and impressions of progress, seeming reluctant to share data. Gathering the right kind of data to monitor shifts in Māori students' achievement was considered challenging in some cases; for example, "So what was the evidence that our teachers were bringing to co-construction, because we thought that that was pretty useless, some of the evidence, and we wanted more, meatier evidence to help our kids." Schools varied in how well they used data. A few facilitators described how the use of data improved the quality of discussion in the group; for example:

> We could go there when we had our co-construction meeting on Monday, 100% of the staff would give evidence to support data to show what they are doing to lift it in the school. And when I first started, when I first had a co-construction meeting it was a disaster and everybody couldn't stand them and so that shift from how the co-construction meetings have changed and no one was bringing data at all, so on Monday everyone was bringing something, I think just signifies a quiet shift in people's thinking: 'I'm going to this meeting, what am I. . ." You know? That puts an onus on them, they have to stand up and front up to what they are doing for Māori students in their classroom and I think there is evidence there for the success of the meeting, would you say?

A Regional facilitator,[1] emphasising that the Te Kotahitanga program challenged established patterns of behaviors within secondary schools, reflected that a greater focus on teacher practice and school systems associated with Māori student achievement data was needed.

> It's such a shift from established patterns of behavior in a secondary context. You know? Why would I bother to talk to an art teacher about my English results? That for a start is a huge break down. There is a journey to travel in it I guess I'd say. I do think that some teams have had less of a handle on that than others. The systems within [some] schools have restricted the configuration of co-construction meetings, so they haven't been able to meet around a core group of students. The conversation becomes much less relevant if I'm just talking to you about what I'm doing, but we don't share students. And so there are challenges in there, some of which are about teacher behavior and teacher practice, some of which about school systems and structures.

In summary, we saw teachers and facilitators actively learning to engage in a partnership with each other, as a way of teachers learning to reposition themselves in relationship to their students, and particularly their Māori students.

The process was often rough; facilitators were perhaps more aware of the rough edges than were the teachers. With the possible exception of shadow-coaching, the great majority of participants found the various elements to the model, and the way they interconnected, to be quite effective and helpful. Also, with few exceptions, the teachers found the facilitators they worked with to be helpful, resourceful, and approachable. The large number of interviews we gathered substantiated the soundness of the model itself as a vehicle for improving classroom practice.

Pedagogical and Cultural Leadership for Enabling Change in the Classroom

Repositioning teachers for culturally responsive pedagogy, using the Te Kotahitanga professional development model, is more than a cycle of activities that people "do." Ultimately, it requires school staff to rethink what teaching and learning are, rethink the notion of expertise and who has it, and re-examine their own identities as racialized people in an unequal society. The job of the facilitation team—leading that learning—requires a good deal of professional knowledge. Below, we discuss various role groups' perceptions of the facilitators and their expertise, then three specific (and overlapping) areas of expertise that facilitators need.

Perceptions of facilitators

In various contexts, the teachers talked about the facilitators, mainly express-ing appreciation for their knowledge, support, and help. We heard words like "fantastic," "incredible," "awesome," "really, really good," "great" and "supportive" used to describe them. Teachers commented mainly on their expertise and support in the classroom. As one put it, "The facilitator is kind of like your on-site expert that teachers never had." Teachers particularly appreciated the facilitators' expertise in teaching and in Māori culture, as well as their resourcefulness. One teacher remarked, "The beauty with the facilitator was like they're trained. They know how to have a professional conversation with you." Another said, "In terms of personal support and so on, . . . and partly in terms of shadow coaching and then also in regular feed-ing of information 'have you tried this? Have you read this article? Here is a copy of it on the e-mail' or something like that. And those things have been quite useful." For the most part, teachers also valued the flexibility and approachability of the facilitators.

A few teachers said they would have liked more balance between Māori and non-Māori facilitators, noting that "there should be more representation of Māori on the facilitation team" because of the importance of expertise in Māori culture. A few also said there was a bit of disconnect when facilitators worked in their school only one or two days per week.

When teachers critiqued facilitators, their main concern was wanting someone with more subject-specific knowledge, who could make a more direct connection to their subject matter, such as graphics, maths, or French. (As secondary teachers, any given facilitator is likely to have taught only 2–3 subjects.) Also, about a half dozen teachers felt that a facilitator they had worked with was too forceful with his or her ideas, "imposing how they think things should be on me." As one teacher put it, "Sometimes I think people get a little bit doctrinaire about things. And lose sight of what I would call common sense." Overall, however, teachers valued the expertise of the facilitators, and found their role and their knowledge central to improving classroom teaching for Māori students.

Principals and other senior/middle managers overwhelmingly agreed that the role of the facilitators and particularly that of the lead facilitator was crucial to the success of Te Kotahitanga. They were also clear that this was a challenging role that didn't suit everyone and that finding and keeping the right person was affected by staffing changes over time. The dispositions, skills, understandings, and even the credibility of the facilitator as someone in the role of supporting other teachers can be an issue.

Facilitators' perceptions of the importance of facilitator expertise

Facilitators are the lynchpin of the work of repositioning teachers in relationship to their students, and particularly their Māori students. We probed them to find out the kind of expertise this work requires. They discussed expertise in three main areas: Māoritanga (socialization and education into the Māori world) and its relationship to culturally responsive classroom pedagogy, subject matter expertise that they can connect with culturally responsive pedagogy, and the process of working with teachers and other adult learners. Facilitators were quite candid in discussing both their knowledge as well as their challenges and limitations in these areas.

Culturally responsive pedagogy and culture

Overwhelmingly, facilitators expressed that the most difficult part of the Te Kotahitanga professional development for teachers and for them as facilitators was the explicit focus on culture and culturally responsive pedagogies, because, as one put it, "It is an enormous amount to come to terms with. You've always got to question, you've always got to unpack." Another commented:

> It's [culturally responsive teaching] also taken a lot of people to quite difficult places with themselves and their practice. So there's been some really challenging, um, interactions, not horrible ones, but, you know, really difficult conversations. Um, for me personally I felt resistance from people that before I was a Facilitator I would never have had. You know there's a, an uncomfortableness. So I guess it's that dissonance stuff. Um, and, and it's good at the end but those are real obvious things, because now it's being talked about and the word Māori is being struggled with. . . . It's like . . . we're not used to that in New Zealand, we're not used to describing a group as Māori. All of those dissonance type interactions are happening.

Facilitators encountered groups of teachers who struggled to understand the importance and impact of relationship-based pedagogies for Māori students. As one facilitator commented, "There are some people who still can't get their head around this whakawhanaungatanga (building relationships)". Facilitators were aware of their need for strong expertise in Māori culture, and the relationship between culture and culturally responsive pedagogies. Because the position of Māori culture within Te Kotahitanga is central to the process of repositioning teachers, some facilitators emphasised a need for their own ongoing development of expertise in Māori culture. Lack of expertise, or discomfort with directly addressing Māori culture, sometimes led to friction within the facilitation team.

An issue that is implicit throughout Te Kotahitanga but not explicit in the model or in most discussions is the cultural identity (Māori vs. non-Māori) and Māori knowledge base of the facilitators. Some facilitators stressed that having Māori strongly visible within the facilitation team lent credibility to the school's commitment to Te Kotahitanga:

> I wanted to make sure we had a Māori led facilitation team—it didn't have to have only Māori facilitators but we think we have broken a bit of a barrier this year as we've got a Māori facilitator, which was really a gap in our team.

Teachers working towards the Effective Teaching Profile need facilitators who are, as one put it, "steeped in Māori tikanga" (culture and customs) and can demonstrate culturally responsive practices. While a lead facilitator may not be Māori nor fluent in Māori, the extent to which the team is bicultural could be crucial to the program's ability to provide teachers who are not bicultural with guidance on things Māori across the curriculum.

The focus on Māori students, and learning to take ownership for Māori underachievement, was particularly challenging for some staff members. Facilitators had to work to maintain that focus rather than allowing shifts to discussions about all students. One facilitator explained,

> The fact that it focuses on Māori students [is] challenging for a lot of our staff, to focus on Māori students. Someone might feel like the others are missing out, so, I think it's challenging to actually sell that to the staff really. The data's showing that [focussing on Māori] is important. National data's saying that this is where the need is.

Another commented, "If it wasn't here, I do wonder whether we would lose that focus on Māori student achievement."

Culturally responsive pedagogy and curriculum

The facilitation teams generally had a strong repertoire of teaching skills, and the great majority of teacher comments about the helpfulness of facilitators underscored their pedagogical knowledge. But as many as half of the facilitation teams saw a need for greater focus on links between curriculum and culturally responsive pedagogies. Making these links requires that facilitators have subject matter expertise in addition to pedagogical knowledge. Teachers working in certain subject areas—maths was named most often—struggled to develop culturally responsive pedagogies aligned with their curriculum area. One facilitator noted, "I've worked in two schools, and the maths department found it the most difficult to work in a different way, start to begin to work in different ways." As will be evident in the next chapter, however, many teachers in maths and science managed to make these connections despite the perceived challenges of doing so.

But facilitators occasionally commented on lacking the subject matter background to help them. For example:

> It could also just be my lack of experience [working with different subject teachers] because I'm an English teacher, and I haven't been thinking, widely in those other cultural contexts for those other subjects. Next year, [I would like to] bring in a teacher with more subject expertise in the science and maths area.

We heard similar concerns from some teachers, who wondered if there might be "culturally neutral" subject areas because they were having difficulty envisioning what culturally responsive pedagogy would look like. For example, a science teacher discussed how difficult it was to conceptualise "bringing the cultural perspective into science. It's quite difficult, depending on what topic you are teaching and how are you going to get the cultural perspective into science." A maths teacher spoke to the need to address culturally responsive pedagogy in a subject-specific way:

It's a blanket program and it doesn't identify enough, in my opinion, that different subjects have different needs and different approaches. Mathematics, for all you may want to do group work and differentiated learning, which we will come back to if you are interested. There is a sense in mathematics where you do have to be the teacher and impart knowledge. And again if you push and say 'all your work has to be in group work' and 'Māori kids will only work if they are in a group with Māori kids' you sort of put that as an absolute. Which is one of the things that we've informally heard, you create barriers.

Facilitator teams also felt stretched supporting and challenging teachers with widely varying levels of teaching expertise. At one end of the spectrum, they felt particularly stretched to figure out how to work with teachers who already had a high level of skill in linking culturally responsive pedagogy with curriculum, given that the program does not differentiate a role that would make use of and further develop their expertise. For example, one facilitator explained:

We have teachers who we call high implementers of Te Kotahitanga. I think the high implementers would possibly like more opportunities to have co-construction meetings, opportunities to bounce ideas and talk about pedagogy. I mean I have been part of co-construction meetings where there have been high implementers who have looked stunned because of comments from other people who aren't high implementers.

At the other end of the spectrum, facilitators were challenged working with teachers who had poor teaching and/or classroom management skills. Sometimes this was viewed as an issue of teacher competence within the school that was not being addressed by the senior management:

We were never, ever designed to be a project that picked up poor [teachers] who weren't managing their classes, that was the end of it. So last year I pulled back a bit and said 'In the end, we cannot do constructive Te Kotahitanga feedback in classrooms that are not managed [and are] simply out of control.' So I wrote to the two people and said 'Look, you need to get some help from specialist teachers, you have got to go to that, [so] you feel like you are able to manage your class better.'

Teacher professional development

Teacher professional development and working with adult learners was a third important area of expertise that facilitators needed, and for which their expertise was uneven. They needed to know how to establish and maintain a supportive, trusting working relationship with teachers while also providing enough challenge to drive teaching practice improvements, which was a delicate balancing act. Although most teacher descriptions of facilitators underscored their ability to do this well, the facilitators themselves were aware of the need to pay attention to building relationships while at the same time offering critical feedback; this theme came up frequently in interviews. For example:

> It's quite a different job to teaching. It's a hard job, handling difficult situations. I made [that teacher] cry. I think we are going into teachers' classrooms and challenging them, and that is a big task.

> Just recently when I was in a challenging situation, it was actually starting to unfold as we were doing the feedback. So it's like, how do I address this, and it got to a place where there was not actually a happy medium. As a result of that, you actually have to step back and I felt that the best thing to do was to step back and have someone else come in and then regroup to get it to that place which is where we have got to now. I don't actually think you can be prepared for it.

The facilitators need to learn to work diplomatically with teachers who are resistant to change, and particularly when confronting deficit views towards Māori students. A couple of them pointed out that Te Kotahitanga is both a philosophy that conflicts with that of some teachers, as well as a set of practices that teachers who are uncomfortable with relationship-based teaching resist. Facilitators—even lead facilitators—come to their roles as colleagues of teacher peers, and yet they are cast in a position of providing technical advice and support to others who may consider they are equally qualified and expert in dimensions of the Effective Teaching Profile. Facilitators spoke openly and often about the challenges of managing the tension between providing encouragement that is culturally safe for teachers while also providing constructive criticism where this is needed. For example:

> A challenge I had when I first started was giving advice to people who I considered tuakana, older than myself, or more experienced than myself as well. I didn't like to tell

people where I think they might need to improve. I'm basically at this stage having to explain to more experienced teachers than myself. I've only been a teacher for the last five years or so, [giving advice to] teachers that have been here for 20 odd years.

Learning to navigate, confront, and attempt to change resistant attitudes whilst still supporting teachers and maintaining relationships requires skill that the facilitators were in the process of learning. One challenge that facilitators often mentioned was learning to work with and offer constructive criticism to teachers who were identified as traditional, older, more experienced and/or had higher status (for example, Heads of Departments) than facilitators. Existing power relationships within departments, coupled with issues of facilitator status could present a challenge to the spread of pedagogical reform.

Supporting the Professional Development Model

All lead facilitators who were interviewed believed it was essential that the school have strong leadership supporting the vision and philosophy of Te Kotahitanga if change is to occur and be sustained within schools. Strong leadership entails vision, ownership and commitment to making a difference to Māori student achievement across the leadership structure.

It was important that the principal was seen to be leading changes within the school. It was also necessary that the facilitation team and senior leadership members work in partnership to achieve desired goals, requiring open, regular communication. One facilitator explained, based on experience, the link between strong principal leadership, active support, and impact on Māori students:

> The original principal had the vision and the strength to say that this is what [he/she] wanted for the school, talked to the board and people like that, advocated strongly for Te Kotahitanga all around the country. In the school, [he/she] put all the structures in place and the funding and made sure everything was here for the program. The [first principal] had such strong beliefs that it was going to make a difference and when the times got really tough could have pulled out or the school could have backed away from the hard decisions, but they made the hard decisions and I believe it paid off in the end. Our results show Māori students are doing better than they were 4 years ago.

Strong support from senior management and heads of department was also considered necessary. Some lead facilitators were adamant that what was needed was ongoing training and upskilling for all school personnel, not just classroom teachers. Without the senior leadership collectively going through a learning process that mirrors the professional learning of teachers, an unevenness in support can result:

> This is the principal's vision, but actually the DPs don't want to be part of this, or even HODs. Often that middle management level is where some of the greatest resistance [occurs], and why would we be surprised? Why would we be surprised that some of these people would start to be a little bit twitchy around something that actually challenges status quo?

The unique hierarchy of secondary schools presents a challenge for a fundamental pedagogical shift towards relational, collaborative, co-constructed work. Facilitators seemed poignantly aware that there were different layers of responsibility in secondary schools that all have an impact on school change and the experiences of students. At times they felt a disconnect between Te Kotahitanga activities driven by the principal's commitment and teacher participation, on the one hand, and the layers of other school leaders with major roles and responsibilities to play in the process and the life of the school.

Conclusion

Our findings emphasized teacher and facilitator appreciation of the professional development model. As a professional development program, Te Kotahitanga seemed to be headed in the right direction on at least two criteria. First, the professional development "went directly to teachers rather than through a 'train the teacher' approach and was delivered by the authors and their affiliated researchers" (Yoon, Duncan, Yu Lee, Scarloss, & Shapley, 2007, p. iv). As Yoon et al. maintain, this school-based and classroom-oriented approach to professional development was one of the critical success factors in the nine best in their extensive review of the evidence on how teacher professional development in the United States affects student achievement. Teachers in our evaluation were highly cognizant of this privilege. The second criterion related to the use of time during the professional development. It needed to be "well organized, carefully structured, purposefully directed and focused on content or pedagogy or both" (Guskey & Yoon, 2009, p. 499). Teachers who were interviewed were appreciative of the support given throughout the professional development process, ranging from the university-based research team, the professional facilitation operating with colleagues 'on the ground' and the support for change from Māori students with whānau/caregivers. A major part of the appeal to teachers was the focused nature of the professional development, that is, improving Māori student achievement through the incorporation of culturally responsive pedagogies of relations.

Data from the evaluation emphasized the 'newness' of such partnership activities as teachers worked with others to improve practice and outcomes for Māori students. Findings also highlighted the fragility of such work, particularly the effort to establish dialogical relationships across established school structures. Understanding the vision and philosophy of Te Kotahitanga and enabling that vision to be evident in practice requires new knowledge, skills and dispositions which enables participants to learn together. Te Kotahitanga presents a significant learning challenge to most mainstream secondary schools not only because it directly challenges traditional, 'taken-for-granted' assumptions about teaching and learning, but also 'what counts' as effective professional development within existing contexts of school hierarchies and power relationships. At the same time, the great majority of teachers and facilitators embraced the professional development process, and were willing to work through rough edges they experienced because the teachers found it so helpful.

Shared reflection, metacognitive activities, dialogue and continued inquiry are essential activities for partners attempting to co-construct a new pedagogy of relations. In culturally responsive schooling contexts, teacher and facilitator collaborative work needs to be viewed as one part of a larger shared social learning activity that supports ongoing improvements in practice and student achievement. It can be tempting to position facilitators and teachers as 'professionals' and 'experts' and discount the importance of the power and impact of student and whānau (family) narratives. But doing so would undercut the entire process of shifting power relations and learning to construct ongoing dialogical relationships with those who historically have been positioned as "less" knowledgeable. This issue will be explored in the concluding chapter.

· 6 ·

CULTURALLY RESPONSIVE PEDAGOGIES ACROSS THE CURRICULUM: WHAT TEACHERS SAY AND DO

Catherine Savage and Rawiri Hindle, Victoria University

Introduction

The main purpose of the Te Kotahitanga project is to shift teachers' views of students away from a deficit view and towards a resource view, and to shift classroom instruction from a transmission model to a more discursive, interactive model that reflects culturally responsive practices. This chapter draws on 318 systematic classroom observations in 22 project schools, 98 comparison observations in 10 non-project schools, and interviews with 150 teachers, 19 heads of departments, 19 deputy principals, 22 deans, and 54 facilitators, to illustrate teachers' implementation of the Effective Teaching Profile (ETP) and teachers' perceptions of how their pedagogy had changed as a result of the professional development program.

In the first section of this chapter, we look at the general impact teachers reported and researchers observed in classrooms as result of participating in the professional development program. After briefly highlighting teachers' reflections on their own perceived changes, we present results from the evaluation team's observations in the classrooms, which indicated that the majority of teachers were implementing the Effective Teaching Profile at either a moderate or high level. The next section looks more deeply at the nature of pedagogical changes we saw and teachers described. These included teacher positioning and their use of co-construction and student-focused pedagogy, teachers showing care for students as culturally located individuals, and teachers monitoring and assessing student learning. Finally we discuss the lack of change in some teachers' practice and perceived challenges associated with this. Teachers' engagement in the professional development program was associated with positive change in both teaching practice and outcomes for students (see Chapter 7); however participants also identified 'ongoing challenges' in their attempts to improve practice and outcomes for Māori students. Teachers perceived as low implementers of the Effective Teaching Profile represented a significant challenge to the reform process.

A crucial question for the evaluation team was: How do we know the extent to which these patterns present a change in teaching practice over the last few years? At the time of the evaluation, the schools had participated in the Te Kotahitanga program for 2 to 4 years. As the evaluation did not run concurrently with the professional development implementation, our in-class observations and interviews could only provide a snapshot in time, rather than a measure of change over time. This meant that to some extent we had to extrapolate based on how teachers reported they had changed, and based on a comparison set of in-class observations in non-project schools.

Impact in Classrooms

Both the in-class observations and teacher interviews demonstrate that the Te Kotahitanga program did indeed change teacher practice. While it was impossible to measure where teachers started and the extent to which the project influenced their changes, as we will show throughout this chapter, teachers clearly articulated the impact of professional development on their practice. This evidence helps us gauge the extent to which the patterns in the observation data represent change due to the program. The schools involved in Te Kotahitanga had also been involved in various other initiatives during this time period, so particular practices observed in classrooms cannot necessarily be attributed to the Te Kotahitanga professional development. However, the perceptions of teachers and other participants as to whether Te Kotahitanga was a key factor affecting teaching and learning in the classroom are relevant and persuasive.

Teacher interviews focused primarily on the impact of the professional development, the extent to which teachers described elements of the Effective

Teaching Profile (ETP) in their classroom practice, and the shifts in their pedagogical understanding. Clearly evident were descriptions of teacher agency for student outcomes, which Bishop et al. (2009) describe as a professional commitment and responsibility to bringing about change in Māori students' educational achievement by accepting professional responsibility for the learning of their students as key. All teachers in the program were able to identify the importance of relationships for learning. Since teachers entered the program at widely varying levels of understanding of culturally responsive pedagogy, however, where they went with that understanding differed markedly. Many teachers went on to extend this discussion of relationships, describing how the focus on a culturally responsive pedagogy of relations meant 'caring for Māori students as culturally located individuals'. For some teachers, the emphasis on developing relationships meant changing their classroom practice, repositioning themselves from holding a 'traditional' teacher-centered role to co-constructing and sharing power with students. These teachers described the process of encouraging student voice and choice in classrooms when they had previously dominated the classroom space with teacher talk, highlighting the relevance of learning activities and their efforts to make connections to students' lives outside the classroom. Other teachers reported changes that were small but nevertheless important for them, such as pronouncing Māori students' names correctly and using some Māori language for class instructions.

> Using Māori greetings. Saying 'Kia ora' to the kids as they come into the class. For me that has been a very new thing, and I've found it quite challenging because my pronunciation is not that great . . . it's improving and the kids are happy to give me feedback. . . I think it helps to build that relationship with the kids. (Teacher)

These diverse outcomes for teachers suggest that professional development for culturally responsive pedagogies may need to accommodate teachers at different starting points of understanding and implementation.

Before examining what teachers said in the interviews, we first show the impact of the professional development program as we saw it in classroom observations.

Implementation of the Effective Teaching Profile

The Effective Teaching Profile (EPT) codifies culturally relevant pedagogy as it was described by Māori students in the narratives of experience (Chapter 2). As we describe how teachers implemented the Effective Teaching Profile, readers should keep in mind clearly that we are describing the extent to which they shifted their pedagogy to make it relevant to their Māori students.

The observation data provided insights into the different levels of teacher implementation of the ETP. Three hundred eighteen (318) classroom observations were conducted and analyzed across curriculum subjects in Years 9–10 classrooms. As described in more detail in Chapter 4, the classroom observation data sheet was developed by core evaluation project personnel. The observers used the data sheet to record basic demographic information, room environment, lesson narrative, Māori curriculum content, evidence of the ETP, and teaching and learning types. These observations were evaluated for implementation of the ETP based on the observational records for each lesson observed. High, moderate, and low implementation levels (including missed opportunities) were coded as specified in Chapter 4. Results were summarized by curriculum subjects across schools, and by school across curriculum subjects, identifying exemplars at different implementation levels. Table 6.1 provides an example of the classroom observations at the three different levels of ETP implementation in visual arts.

Nearly 3 out of 4 teachers in project schools evidenced either moderate or high implementation of the Effective Teaching Profile as assessed using our observation measure. But as many as 1 in 4 teachers did not master these dimensions sufficiently and were not implementing the ETP according to the professional development activities provided. Given that this finding is consistent across schools, it would appear that, while the Te Kotahitanga professional development program helped many teachers develop a more culturally responsive pedagogy for their Māori students, alone it may not be sufficient to ensure that all teachers learn to do so.

Interestingly, the difference between schools' onset of and length of participation in the Te Kotahitanga project was not significant. The teachers we observed across the schools in the second year of participation and after four years of participation were operating at similar levels of the Effective Teaching Profile. Clearly, many teachers will have previously mastered some of these dimensions through having learned good teaching as well as through other professional development activities, so no attempt is made to attribute everything we saw to Te Kotahitanga. However, the higher levels of implementation and the richness of the examples emerging from our observation data suggest that Te Kotahitanga is associated with establishing strategies for teaching Māori students effectively.

In October 2009, we were able to carry out 102 classroom observations in four subject areas—English, mathematics, science and social studies—in

Table 6.1 Examples of different levels of implementation in visual arts

	High Implementers	Implementers	Low Implementers
Classroom Description	The posters on the walls are rich in Māori motif including kowhaiwhai, tukutuku and whakairo (patterns). The posters of artwork include Robyn Kahukiwa (artist) and images of harakeke (flax), kete, kahu and hinaki (woven products).In many of the examples the student artwork also has elements of Māori motif. At the beginning of the lesson the teacher encourages the students to keep confident and focused on completing the portfolio by the end of the week.	Student artwork is posted on the walls. Several art books are scattered around, some are on Māori art. Classroom doesn't have obvious front or teacher station. Teacher roams around room talking with students. Students move around room as needed to get materials, and to look at someone else's work. Learning intentions and success criteria are posted on a whiteboard at front of classroom.	There is Māori art everywhere in the room but the lesson made no reference to Māori concepts or content. There are 15 Māori students in the class and 7 non-Māori and the teacher is of European ethnicity. The teacher greets the class with good afternoon, tells them to sit down and gives the instructions for the lesson from the front of the class.
Manaakitanga: (Cares for students as culturally located individuals)	There is a student who has the role of D.J. who is responsible for providing the music for the lesson. The teacher lets the students know that she is free over the lunch break if any of them want to come back and work on their portfolio. The teacher encourages students who are already finished to help the other students. She reinforces student efforts with terms such as, "Your work is looking awesome".	Students appear to have quite a bit of freedom of expression in posters. Teacher sometimes sits with students when talking about work. Students can help each other although most tend to sit at their desk. Some listen to music with earphones while they work.	Not evident in the lesson. Students work on tasks as directed at desks. Students are quiet throughout lesson and do not interact with teacher other than listening and responding to instructions.
Wānanga: (Engage in discursive interactions and facilitates student to student interactions)	The teacher mostly interacts with the students on a one to one basis talking about their artwork and relating this to the learning intentions. She asks open ended questions and encourages the students to expand on their answers. She asks the students what they like about their work and what they could change about it. There is no evidence of student to student interactions.	Teacher discusses one on one artwork, questions students about their work, gives praise for work. Students hang work on wall when complete.	There are no examples in the lesson. All of the teaching is instructional from the front of the room.
Ako: (Use range of strategies to facilitate learning interactions)	Positive reinforcement is the teacher's main strategy. She is quiet spoken and moves around the classroom interacting with the students on a one to one basis asking questions about their artwork. She encourages the students to self-reflect.	Teacher gives students feedback on work, she praises effort and art. Teacher talked to students about next steps. Students are engaged in learning and follow strong routines.	The teacher did not demonstrate what to do to achieve the desired effects for the art. He told them to use multi-media and a variety of materials. There was no discussion about this or demonstration.

Table 6.2 Effective Teaching Profile (ETP) evidence at schools in English, mathematics, science and social studies: Percentages and numbers of observations rated at different levels of implementation

Level of Implementation	Post-Implementation Schools (N = 195*)	Pre-Implementation Schools (N = 98**)
Low	24% (46)	47% (46)
Moderate	50% (98)	48% (47)
High	26% (51)	5% (5)

* Numbers reflect observations conducted in only the 4 named subjects at these schools.
** Of the total of 102 observations at Phase 5 schools, 4 were invalid and could not be scored (e.g., students sitting a test).
The original source for Table 6.2 and Figure 6.1 is: Catherine Savage, Rawiri Hindle, Luanna H. Meyer, Anne Hynds, Wally Penetito, & Christine E. Sleeter (2011). Culturally responsive pedagogies in the classroom: indigenous student experiences across the curriculum. *Asia-Pacific Journal of Teacher Education*, 39:3, 183-198. http://www.tandfonline.com.

10 of 17 additional schools that had not yet begun the project at the time (pre-implementation). This group provided a valid and representative sample for comparison purposes, as a baseline to assess growth on the ETP for teachers in participating schools. Table 6.2 summarizes the levels of implementation for these schools. As observations were only carried out in the four subject areas in pre-implementation schools, the comparison observations from the project schools (post-implementation) were restricted to English, mathematics, science and social studies for this analysis.

These data show significant differences in the percentages of teachers demonstrating high and low levels of implementation of the ETP. In the project schools, 1 in every 4 teachers are "high implementers", whereas approximately 1 in 4 teachers are "low implementers." This contrasts sharply with the pre-implementation schools where nearly half of the teachers demonstrate low implementation and only 5% demonstrate high implementation of the ETP prior to Te Kotahitanga professional development program. It appears that the program halved the proportion of low implementers and increased the proportion of high implementers many times over, demonstrating significant impact of the professional development on teacher classroom practice.

Implementing the ETP across the curriculum

In interviews some teachers told us they believed culturally responsive pedagogies were more challenging to implement in their classroom because of the subject they taught.

Table 6.3 Effective Teaching Profile (ETP) results by subject area across schools (N=318)

Subject Area(s)	Total observations	Lesson numbers (and percentages) by quality category		
		Low Implementation	Implementation	High Implementation
Arts, Drama, Music, Dance	35	7 (20%)	19 (54%)	9 (26%)
Business, Commerce, Super Studies	8	3 (38%)	4 (50%)	1 (12%)
English	59	18 (31%)	26 (44%)	15 (25%)
Health & Physical Education	18	5 (27%)	9 (50%)	4 (23%)
Japanese & Spanish	7	2 (16%)	3 (42%)	2 (16%)
Te reo Māori	9	0	4 (44%)	5 (55%)
Maths	48	6 (13%)	29 (60%)	13 (33%)
Science	49	15 (31%)	24 (49%)	10 (20%)
Social Studies	39	7 (18%)	19 (48%)	13 (33%)
Technology/ IT/Graphics	26	4 (15%)	10 (38%)	6 (23%)
Totals	318	77 (24%)	157 (49%)	84 (26%)

That is what has been so difficult in science, bringing the cultural perspective into science. It's quite difficult, depending on what topic you are teaching and how are you going to get the cultural perspective into science. It's quite difficult there. (Teacher)

Yeah, in maths it's difficult [to integrate culturally responsive pedagogies]. (Teacher)

The evaluation team was interested to see if variations in subject areas were evident in the data. Table 6.3 shows an analysis of teachers' implementation of the ETP across different curriculum areas.

In schools implementing Te Kotahitanga, the highest percentage of high implementation exemplars was observed in Te reo Māori (Māori language) (55%), although for a small sample of only 9 observations. Both mathematics and social studies show positive patterns, with high percentages of teachers operating at both high and moderate implementation and only 6 (11%) maths observations and 7(18%) social studies observations operating at the low implementation level. Of the 59 observations in English, one-quarter of teachers were operating at the high implementation level with another 44% at the moderate implementation level of the ETP. Science classrooms demonstrated similar patterns of implementation as English, both groups having a significant proportion of low implementers (31%). Table 6.3 demonstrates that while there were some variances in the data, all subject areas evidenced high, moderate and low implementers, demonstrating that culturally responsive pedagogy is not subject specific. Interestingly there were patterns in individual school data suggesting that particularly skilled subject facilitators or teachers in middle management may influence the outcome in individual schools.

Dimensions of Culturally Responsive Pedagogies in the Classroom

There were three major ways in which teachers' practice changed as a result of their engagement in the Te Kotahitanga professional development. These are: teachers' positioning and development of co-construction and student-focused classrooms, teachers caring for students as culturally located individuals, and teachers' monitoring and assessment of student learning. We intersperse examples from teacher interviews with in-class observation data to illustrate how teacher descriptions of these changes were evident in classroom practice.

Change in teacher positioning, co-construction and student-focused classrooms

Implementation of the Effective Teaching Profile requires teachers to reposition themselves from a traditional teacher-centered role to co-constructing and sharing power with students. Bishop et al. (2009) claim that a classroom where the teacher using culturally responsive pedagogy as reflected in the Effective Teaching Profile "will generate totally different interaction patterns and educational outcomes from a classroom where knowledge is seen as something that the teacher makes sense of and then passes onto students and will be conducted within and through pedagogy of relations, wherein self-determining individuals interact with one another within non-dominating relations of interdependence" (p. 741). In the analysis of the interview data we sought to understand how teachers perceived their role in the teaching and learning process.

We found that teachers talked about 'repositioning' themselves in the classroom. They described this process as a move away from being the traditional 'expert' whereby teachers were viewed as the 'font of all knowledge' and used 'chalk and talk methods' to convey knowledge to students. Across schools teachers described an increased attempt to involve actively students in the teaching and learning process. According to the teachers, repositioning involved negotiation and co-construction of learning and behavior strategies, whereby student voice was welcomed and acknowledged.

> It was a paradigm shift between what you (as a teacher) perceive as power or control or authority in the classroom, you don't lose that by sharing it, and I think that was a major paradigm shift. You don't actually become weaker; you become a stronger teacher by sharing it [power with students]. (Head of Department)

Teachers reported developing more discursive teaching approaches that Bishop et al. (2009) posit are necessary to enhance student motivation, engagement and achievement. Some emphasized the shift to more 'student focused' classrooms whereby students were expected to take responsibility for their own and others' learning and behavior. Teachers spoke about experimentation with paired, group and cooperative learning activities. Teachers discussed the importance of co-construction approaches and described negotiating with students to get their input into processes used in the classroom. They identified that this strategy engaged and motivated Māori students, as well as enabling them to care for students as culturally located individuals.

> I think it's important that students have that input into their own learning and we've done a project based on a Māori sculptor. And part of that project, I integrated the Māori students into helping me to come up with that project and asking them, what would be really a good project for you to do that would be interesting for you? And I think it was one of the most successful projects that we've done this year, and that came from the students. (Teacher)

Many participants explained the difference that engaging in the Te Kotahitanga professional development had made to teachers creating more student-focused classrooms. A key strategy for developing such a classroom climate was through paired activities and cooperative group learning. Teachers commonly reported learning through such experiences that students were often 'the best teachers' for their peers, and many school personnel described this process as a profound change. Through describing these changes in their classroom practice, teachers emphasized that they had learned about the value of structuring learning activities where students were expected to learn from each other. At times this had been an uneasy process for some teachers, who had not previously used these strategies:

> I used to be very put off by doing group work, because I was much more goal-orientated, and holding individuals accountable for what I wanted done now, and I push my thing from the front. Working in groups didn't gel for me in terms of the kinds of things I was stressing about. And as soon as I found out about it I thought, oh, this is going to be a huge waste of my time, having to sit back, and structure groups, and then allow them to work in groups, and provide them with some resource material, maybe assistance, just facilitate for them, but leave them to it, to a much greater extent than I normally would. I would want to be intervening there, much more. And I found the fact that I could actually leave, that—well, for me personally—that I could change my methodology. But then, to see them respond, and then later when I look at the results and the work, you know, even when we do pieces of individual work further down the line and I then I go back and I say well, this is great, where did you get this from, and they said oh, it came out in the discussion, during that day when we were working in groups. (Teacher)

This shift in classroom dynamics and the type of interaction patterns between teachers and students was further evident in the observation data, which revealed that the type of classroom activity changed depending on the teachers' levels of ETP implementation. In the classroom observations, we recorded how much time was spent in the following pedagogical formats: students working in small groups, teacher elaborating on ideas, teacher presenting factual material, students doing seatwork, and non-academic use of time. Figure 6.1 demonstrates how the implementation level of the Effective Teaching Profile dictated what the students experienced.

Students in classrooms of teachers we rated as high implementers of the Effective Teaching Profile spent more than a quarter of their learning time in small group work. These groups were organized using cooperative strategies with role assignments and clearly identified task outcomes. Teachers supported the groups by asking questions and requiring students to elaborate. In high implementation classrooms, less time was spent in seatwork, non-academic transitions, and socializing unrelated to learning.

In classrooms where teachers were moderate implementers of culturally response pedagogies as reflected on the Effective Teaching Profile, students

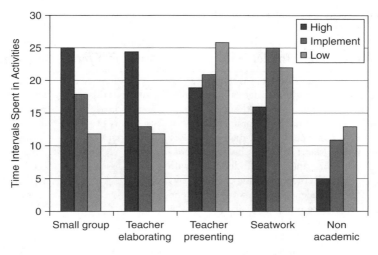

Figure 6.1 Analysis of activity time across five kinds of activity in high implementation, moderate implementation and low implementation classrooms.

spent more time completing individual seatwork than students in classrooms of high implementers, but they also spent time in small group work. Compared with high implementers, moderate implementers spent more teacher talk time presenting facts rather than elaborating with higher order questions, and students spent more time in non-academic activities, socializing and transitions, and less time in student-led activities.

In classrooms of teachers we rated as low implementers, students spent nearly half of their time in individual seatwork or listening to teachers presenting facts. A significant proportion of time involved non-academic transitions and socializing, and management challenges were at a level likely to interfere with learning. Only a tenth of the learning time was spent working in small groups, and there were only 6 student-led activities across all the low implementation observations. Teachers who were low implementers did not explicitly state learning objectives or success criteria, nor set high expectations for students. Some teachers seemed unable to demonstrate positive relationships with Māori students while maintaining classroom discipline. There were fewer discursive practices, student experiences were not referenced, and there was less variety in teaching and learning activities.

In Table 6.4, we illustrate classroom practice across a range of implementers of mathematics lessons. The left column lists the 6 dimensions of the Effective Teaching Profile (we clustered some of them), and the next 3 columns draw

Table 6.4 Teaching exemplars for the Effective Teaching Profile in mathematics

ETP Dimensions	High Implementers	Moderate Implementers	Low Implementers
Care for students as culturally located individuals	Greets students as they enter, shows knowledge of individual students asking them about Kapahaka (cultural performance) festival, rugby, etc. Uses Māori greeting when approaching and talking individually with all students during class. Sits by students, relates work to student interests (rugby) and puts maths problem in context discussed with students.	Only reference to culture is relating worksheet to Treaty of Waitangi.	Teacher introduces observer from Victoria University, says "You may end up going there, I believe they need cleaners"; later apologizes for remark.
Discursive teaching and learning & Use of a range of strategies to facilitate learning interactions	Student leads activity, explains maths problem to class, demonstrates to whole class. Teacher manages class but has students run groups working on maths problems, emphasizes "helping each other make a plan for excellence". Teacher moves around groups, participating.	Primarily Q&A from the whiteboard, giving students time to try then doing the equation together.	Teacher directs entire lesson from front, students told to keep quiet and work on task individually; sends students out of room for talking aloud; no discussion.
High expectations for student learning & Promote, monitor and reflect learning outcomes with students	Shares goal of class regarding achieving level 3 Merit and Excellences, writes 'confidence' on the board by the learning outcomes and explains importance of confidence when sitting exams, explains marking system and importance of reasoning. Whole class agrees on evaluation of work against learning objective.	Teacher expects all students to complete the measurement task and checks on their work, giving help as needed. Learning outcomes are posted but the purpose of the activity not explained.	No learning outcomes posted or described by the teacher, and no expectations for student work are given. Instead, students are given an assignment to work on individually during class.
Manage class to promote learning	Explains about co-construction meeting the previous day and the goal teachers agreed upon for their class. Shared how they would be working towards encouraging students to take leadership roles and develop confidence of all members in class. Gives positive feedback about this when student leads solution to maths problem on board.	Teacher primarily responds to hands up asking for help or intervenes when it is obvious student/s not working on the assigned task.	Students continue talking out of turn despite being asked several times to be quiet; student sent out of the class to stand outside the door during observation.

examples from classroom observations that illustrate each dimension (or missed opportunities for using that dimension). What is apparent is that the degree to which teachers' pedagogy reflecting the ETP dictated the type of activity students were engaged with in the classroom and the extent to which they were required to participate actively. Clearly the ETP is a sound pedagogical tool, and its implementation increases the degree to which students are actively engaged in their own learning. Teachers identified this as being the shift they made in their own classroom practice. While many found it challenging to shift the balance of power in the classroom, the observation data demonstrated that the majority of teachers were able to do this successfully.

Change in teachers caring for students as culturally located individuals

A focus for all teachers in interviews was the importance of making and maintaining positive relationships with students and demonstrating care for student learning. Caring for students as culturally located individuals within a framework of positive student-teacher relationships is considered beneficial for all students, but particularly so for Māori (Bishop et al., 2003; Hall & Kidman, 2004). Caring, as understood in this context, goes beyond simple feelings of affect. Valenzuela (1999) distinguished between aesthetic caring, which involves affective expression only, and authentic caring, which entails deep reciprocity and, in the case of teachers, taking responsibility for providing an education environment in which their students thrive. This kind of caring entails getting to know students, attending to student input regarding teaching and learning, respecting students' intellectual abilities, and valuing identities students bring into school from home. As such, an important part of establishing and maintaining positive relationships with Māori students involves the ways in which teachers value, respect and include Māori students' cultural knowledge in the classroom. This meant teachers learning to use a variety of concepts and materials that students could relate to and that were familiar to them.

> [It is most important] In my subject relating, using what they have got, for example in this community using Māori knowledge and resources to reinforce concept. For example in level 1 NCEA when we did transformation, rotation, reflecting—and I used a Māori design—kids love drawing Māori design, they did research around Māori design—had to relate them to transformation, reflection, rotation. Using what they have at home—using their knowledge they're really into it. As a result 95% of them passed the assessment. (Teacher)

As mentioned in above, students were able to participate and lead learning in many classrooms of moderate and high implementers. Observers witnessed teachers asking students what they wanted to study, such as students suggesting films they might like to study in a film study unit, or students writing their own lesson plans for the class. Student knowledge was incorporated in a variety of ways across the subject areas. For example, in a cooking class students had brought recipes from home and cooked in groups, each teaching the others how to cook their dish. In an English class students were encouraged to use their own experiences and to include their whānau (family) in their writing. In an art class students were asked to reflect on how they saw themselves in relation to their art. Teachers considered student interest in lesson planning, using hooks to engage students in learning, for example, clips from a popular New Zealand cartoon Bro Town, YouTube clips, and even a *CSI* video clip in a science lesson about flies.

In many classrooms where the ETP was implemented, Māori protocols were evident, such as karakia (prayer) and whakatauki (proverbs), which could be seen displayed in the classroom and in some cases referred to during the lesson. Observation data evidenced the use of Te Reo Māori (the Māori language) in many classrooms, and where some teachers found pronunciation of Māori names and words as difficult, they asked students for help. As an example this teacher asked:

> "Please tell me if I don't pronounce this word correctly" (she attempts the word) and a Māori student replies: "Miss, that was good". (observation)

The interview data supported these observations, as teachers discussed using te reo, and how attempting to correctly pronounce Māori names and words had led to an improvement in teacher-student relationships. In all cases, teachers reported that students appreciated their attempts at using te reo.

> I go into a classroom and I say "Kia ora" and the response is brilliant, you know they go "Kia ora Miss" and I would never have done that before and it's just made me think. . . . I think it just taught me basic words to use and you know they appreciate that, they really appreciate that and I guess I wouldn't have necessarily done that beforehand. (Teacher)

In the interviews, several teachers discussed how the professional development had impacted on their personal learning in relation to Māori concepts like mana (the essence or reality of a being) and manaakitanga (caring for students as cultural located), and how they saw this manifesting in their classroom practice. It appears as though learning these Māori concepts had informed some teachers' values and beliefs and led to a better understanding of biculturalism and the place of the partnership between Māori and others in New Zealand, as the following example illustrates:

> I've found it really important to personally take on some of the Māori terminology and the mana framework, and I also think that when I'm engaging with particular students, those central Māori concepts . . . things like manaakitanga, So . . . you are going right back to the treaty in the sense that you've got both the European and the Māori framework operating side by side. . . . And just and awareness of the fact that Māori students are tangatawhenua (local people) and the way that I'd approach them. So increasingly I'm finding myself thinking in that kind of bicultural way while still carrying on a lot of the practices. But it's kind of got a focus and clarity to it that I wouldn't have necessarily had before. (Teacher)

Being culturally located is not only about things Māori but also about acknowledging students as part of their own cultural world. Students' cultural identities are multifaceted and are constructed for many students around sports, music, friends, outside interests, as well as cultural affiliations. Analysis of the observation data evidenced that teachers who were implementing culturally responsive pedagogy demonstrated positive relationships with students and expressed an interest in students' lives outside of the classroom. Teachers knew students well as they interacted with them, asking about cultural and sporting activities, such as, "How did you do at the Kapahaka festival?" or acknowledging students' favorite TV program: "You can solve this math problem tonight after you watch The Crowd Goes Wild". Teachers asked after students, friends and family, and shared information about themselves. For example, in one classroom a student asked a teacher what he did during the weekend, and the teacher replied "My nephews stayed at my house". Teachers reported that reciprocity, with teachers sharing their own lives and interests, was important in establishing positive trusting relationships in the classroom. Again this was viewed as a form of teacher repositioning, as moving away from 'the traditional teacher who did not smile until Easter'. In this way students could also reciprocate by letting the teacher know more about their lives and interests outside of the classroom. Reciprocal sharing was considered useful in creating learning activities that were relevant to Māori students:

> It's also about sharing a bit of me as the teacher. . . so that they feel comfortable sharing some of their own knowledge and experiences from outside of the classroom with me. . . and that's important knowledge to have because I can use that in my teaching

to link into things that they are familiar with, and their prior knowledge. So it's also creating learning contexts that they are familiar with. (Teacher)

In contrast, teachers who were low implementers were more likely to be very passive, or when engaging with the students, let social talk dominate the classroom. In some cases, teachers were found to be confrontational with students, as an example from one classroom observation when a student initiated a conversation with a teacher the teacher responded, "We're not here for social bonding, we're here for learning".

In classroom observations, we noted that many of the teachers implementing the Effective Teaching Profile saw themselves as part of the classroom learning community using language like 'we' and referring to the entire class as 'whānau'. A New Zealand term, whānau is often used to describe genealogical family, but can also be used to describe group relationships; for example, Kaupapa (agenda) whānau refers to a group of people coming together for a common purpose like a sports team or cultural group. Teachers used whānau in this context to describe the class. The tone of these classrooms was often kept light as teachers allowed students to share a joke, to laugh, and often used appropriate humor in their teaching. As an example, in a maths class teaching probability, the teacher said:

"What's the probability of me marrying Brad Pitt?" A student replies," Zero!" The class and teacher laugh and the teacher continues, "What's the probability of it raining in Auckland?" (observation)

Teachers who did not implement the ETP tended to display relationships with students that were under significant tension and stress. Approximately half the low implementers demonstrated confrontational behavior, threatening students with detention or to tell their parents how they behaved. Teacher voices were often raised and the language used ('you' and 'I') tended to separate the students from the teachers; demonstrated by these examples of the language used in classrooms by low implementing teachers:

"Look I am really getting annoyed with you". (observation)

"Hey, cut it out now, stop talking, don't mess with me". (observation)

"There has been too much messing around, if you're finished I have something else for you to do—we will be waiting in at lunchtime, get your hats off my lesson hasn't finished this has been appalling". (observation)

The remaining low implementers tended to be passive and ignore progressively challenging behavior in the classroom. Although many of these low implementing teachers interacted with students in a positive way individually, they did not manage the classroom for learning.

Changes in teacher monitoring and related assessment activities

Many teachers described having increased their monitoring of Māori students' on-task behavior and their use of new assessment activities, such as explicit use of learning intentions, feedback and feed-forward. Of central importance is teachers being better able to identify their Māori students in class. Many times teachers told us that before participating in the Te Kotahitanga program, they did not know who their Māori students were and/or how they were doing in their classrooms. Teachers talked about being able to better identify their Māori students as a key expectation of their engagement in the professional development program. Identifying Māori students in class was essential and linked to broader monitoring and related assessment activities. For example, we observed teachers circulating more around the classroom in order to monitor Māori students' work and engagement better. Teachers explained that they made more of an effort to clarify the learning and achievement focus for students.

> Being aware of making the students more aware of what they're learning, hence the learning intentions. But my success criteria doesn't come from myself, I'm more about the kids, so I try to ask "well, how are we going to learn this?" and they usually come up with it. (Teacher)

> Today we were looking at a formative assessment. There are summative assessments still about four weeks away. But we needed to them to find out [how they're doing] now. And what they need to work on before that summative assessment. They knew that before the class and they'd been preparing for it and were quite excited about it. The task then was for each of these small groups within the class to come up with their personal style on delivering the same script which was the chorus piece from Romeo and Juliet right at the beginning of the play. To focus them, we had a recap, to make sure that everybody was on board, knew exactly what had been done up to that point. (Teacher)

High implementing teachers displayed learning objectives that were related to learning and referred to these in the lesson. Success criteria were often identified on the whiteboard and in some cases co-constructed with students. Consider the examples in Table 6.5 across a couple of subject areas. Clearly, high implementing teachers required students to reflect on their own

Table 6.5 High implementing exemplars of the effective teaching profile

ETP	English	Mathematics
Caring for students as culturally located	Teacher greets students 'Morena' as they come in room. Encourages students to write their magazine article about their own culture, their whānau– asks them to "bring your own knowledge to the task". Students use Te Reo in the class to each other and teacher.	Greets students at door, shows knowledge of individual students as he asks them about Kapahaka festival, rugby. Uses Māori greeting when approaching and talking individually with all students in the period. Sits by students, relates work to student interest (rugby) and puts math problem in the context discusses with student.
Discursive teaching and learning. Using a range of strategies to facilitate	Co-operative structures think pair share students share reflection students asked to critique to agree/ disagree with peer and highlight evidence for their judgments. Gives student choice about way of working. SEEP strategy (statements, explanation, example, personal evaluation) for student reflection. Teacher conferencing with individuals about work while group working.	Student lead activity explains math problem to class and demonstrates to whole class. Teacher manages class but uses students to run groups working on math problems, emphasis on "helping each other make a plan for excellence". Teacher moves around groups participating.
High expectations for learning and promote, monitor and reflect learning outcomes with students	Teacher says, "We are a whānau and we need to care about one another's success, we are here to help each other". Teacher sets class goal that all students will get at least achieved in English exams. Finishes lesson by asking students to describe biggest change you have to make in terms of your work/progress towards these English exams, asks students to reflect on how far they've come.	Shares goal of class regarding achieving level 5 merit and excellences, writes confidence on the board by the LO and explain importance of confidence when sitting exams, explain marking system importance of reasoning. Whole class agrees on evaluation of class work against LO.
Manage class to promote learning	Teacher encourages students, individually checks student engagement on task. Teacher emphasizes choice and responsibility. Quiet one to one conversations with students informally getting them to help one another in their group. Praises positive behavior and highlights learning.	Explains about co-construction meeting held the night before and the goal teachers had agreed upon for class, Shared how they would be working towards encouraging students to take leadership roles and developing confidence of all members in class. Gives positive feedback about this when student takes lead and teaches class math problem on board.

learning, asking students' opinions of their work and asking them what they needed to know to move forward. In some cases the success criteria were used for personal reflection at the end of the lesson, or to construct their own reflective questions which they answered using the criteria. In contrast, the learning outcomes in low implementing classrooms tended to describe the activity rather than the learning, for example: "To make a blinky board". Or, they were not evident in the classroom at all.

The observation data demonstrated that the nature of the classroom learning talk differed depending on the teacher's level of implementation of the Effective Teaching Profile. Teachers who were high implementers actively involved students in problem solving, encouraging debate between students, and asking for evidence to support discussion. Rather than telling students how to solve problems, teachers posed questions to students like, "Any ideas about how we can go achieve this?" There were several instances where teachers took a not knowing position, asking who could help or putting students in the role of the teacher by asking, "Can someone tell me how to do that as I'm not sure?" Teachers who were high implementers were more likely to engage students in discussion rather than talking at them; for example: "Before I give you my opinion, tell me what you think about this".

In contrast, the talk of teachers who were low implementers tended to be heavily focused on issuing behavioral instructions and setting tasks such as worksheets which could be completed individually. Whole class discussions in low implementing classrooms lacked focus and in some cases were described as chaotic by observers. This was supported by interview data as teachers discussed their realization that Māori students would achieve if classroom instruction is engaging, and that through the Te Kotahitanga observation and feedback process they became aware that they have the power to make this happen:

> Student engagement is at the core of the observation. I mean, there's the vast array of things that is observed, but student engagement is probably the one you focus very much on. In a way, starting with the student as opposed to what the teacher does, it's pretty hard to argue with that, if they're not engaged they're not going to learn, so they're not going to achieve so in a way it is starting with the student and then working backwards, 'how are we [going to] engage them more' as opposed to saying 'here's a brilliant idea let's all go and do.' (Teacher)

When discussing assessment in the classroom, high and moderate implementers of the Effective Teaching Profile often set high expectations and made reference to the national assessment system (NCEA). Many teachers explained the NCEA credit system in the context of the lesson, telling that, "You need to do (explanation) in order to get a merit or an excellence". Classroom tasks were related to assessment activities, students were given feedback based on assessment and given positive feedback regarding exam sitting skills, such as "Geez, you're good you'll pass that question". In many of these classrooms, students were gaining early NCEA credits, and teachers had high expectations and viewed assessment as a team effort, stating, for example: "We need to make a plan for excellence, we need to have confidence—go out of our comfort zone and take leadership that's our focus". There was a strong sense of collaboration and collegiality in the classroom with teachers using language that included themselves in the group; for example, teachers said things like, "We're a great team!" "We can do this!" There was a strong sense of reliance on each other to achieve: "We are a whānau—so we need to care about each other's success . . . we need to help and challenge each other to get through these exams, we need to get serious". Students were directed to help one another: "If you finished, help someone who isn't, help others to achieve".

Ongoing Challenges—A Lack of Change in Some Classrooms

Teachers' engagement in the professional development program was perceived to have enabled positive change in both practice and outcomes for Māori students across project schools. Nevertheless, participants also identified 'ongoing challenges' in the attempt to improve practice and outcomes for Māori students. The majority of teachers who were interviewed were positive and enthusiastic about the impact of Te Kotahitanga in classrooms and schools. They understood the components of the program and were able to articulate how this had informed their classroom practice. However, a key challenge for many school leaders and facilitators was how to prompt change in classrooms of teachers who were perceived as 'low implementers' across schools. While there may be contextual influences in each school that produced variances, such as the availability of subject-related expertise in culturally responsive pedagogies, cultural knowledge, and leadership commitment, every school had low implementing teachers. Across the schools, we rated approximately 1 in every 4 teachers as a low implementer. While these teachers were not demonstrating culturally responsive pedagogies, they also communicated low or no expectations for student achievement, failed to state learning outcomes, and evidenced poor classroom management alongside high percentages of non-academic use of classroom time. A key challenge for schools is how to address teachers who are non-performing.

In interviews, a small minority of teachers felt that the program's explicit focus on Māori students was unnecessary since they saw Te Kotahitanga as just basic good teaching:

> I think it's the same with what would work for any student achievement: clear objectives, clear instructions, interesting subject content, and good relationship with the teacher, I think. I'd say it's the same for any pupil. (Teacher)

In a few cases this view was more virulent as teachers saw the focus on Māori as separatist, with one or two teachers going so far as to identify the project's focus on Māori students as being divisive, illustrated by the following view that all students should be treated the same:

> I'm going to say [what's] probably going to be a negative thing, I find it really hard that it's only for Māori students. And I do that for all my students, it doesn't matter if they're boys or girls, if they're Samoan, Tongan, Nuiean or Māori. (Teacher)

Such views would inhibit a teacher's ability to assume agency to address Māori underachievement purposely. Although some teachers felt this may be a belief that dissipates over time, some teachers may struggle to make the connections necessary to implement a change in practice.

> A lot of people, especially initially, were concerned that it was positive discrimination of a nature that was going to not benefit others. But so many years down the track, I think the benefits from the small group that it's targeting is huge and there are the ramifications do spread out to the rest of the class and the school, ultimately.

Clearly, teachers were starting at different places with respect to their knowledge of culturally responsive pedagogies as expressed by the ETP.

Other misconceptions existed as teachers found the move to a more discursive mode of practice conflicting with many of their beliefs regarding 'good teaching'. While all teachers considered it important that teachers make the effort to get to know their Māori students, several emphasized that this could not be at the expense of high expectations, as though these things were a binary. For example, the following teacher described the challenge she felt in developing high expectations alongside positive relationships:

> Sure if you have a positive working relationship it helps, but you need to, as the teacher, you need to have clear and high expectations for the kids, don't threaten things that you're not going to follow up on, you need to have clear consequences for things and that's not just for Māori kids that' for all kids.(Teacher)

Such teachers held a fundamental misconception about learning and behavior and the place of relational pedagogy, that is, that having positive relationships means to be 'friends' and that teachers cannot be too friendly if they are to manage learning and maintain the power. Observations indicated that high implementers did not compromise high expectations or behavioral standards in the classroom for positive relationships, and that these elements of the ETP could co-exist. It was apparent from the classroom observations and teacher interviews that classroom management practices needed to change as teachers learned to implement culturally responsive pedagogy, and that some teachers struggled with this. Based on the classroom observations, we found that more than 80% of the classrooms of teachers who were low implementers were mismanaged. These teachers who struggled with major classroom management issues were an identified group that facilitators found demanding and in fact felt were out of their control.

> Acknowledging that there are some situations that are above you (as a Facilitator), like major classroom management issues. (Facilitator)

Nevertheless, although few in number, these teachers did exist in project schools and without a doubt had considerable effect on the learning of both Māori and non-Māori students. Subsequent iterations of Te Kotahitanga have taken this into account by examining the place of pedagogical leadership in leading change for teachers clearly not managing their classrooms.

A further challenge appeared to be addressing the ongoing professional learning of teachers in the schools. As teachers progressed and moved through the cycle of observations and feedback, goal setting and coaching, they identified professional learning needs that they felt could not be addressed by the program. A particular challenge appeared to be related to the teaching of specialist subject areas and the resources available to them as they worked to develop more culturally responsive pedagogies:

> I need to bring more cultural aspects into my teaching. You know look for things that could apply, which is not always easy, because sometimes I go in the chemistry route in the senior years, it's just trying to find some good cultural [resources]. . . . And to

quite academic subjects, like when you are doing construction of the atom and you are doing protons, electrons and neutrons, it gets quite hard. (Teacher)

For some, this lack of content knowledge from facilitators had led to teachers considering other ways that they might fulfil this need as described by the teacher below. Access to subject content knowledge was a recurring theme across the project schools indicating that schools could investigate establishing subject-specific learning communities. These comments further support the notion of pedagogical leaders in schools, particularly in the middle management areas.

(Asking them about their culture and sharing with the class) . . . One of the things we were, among ourselves talking about, is how helpful it would be for somehow, either the subject area professional associations or something, help on the website or in books or something, so teachers could see subject specific ways. . . . I would also like to see more people in my area of region taking part in TK so we can meet and share ideas, just to get it a bit more established as well, and ideas flowing. And then obviously I wouldn't have the issue I have with my mentors at the moment which is a bit of a subject barrier. (Teacher)

Different teachers and facilitators across schools also perceived that if facilitators had specific expertise and previous teaching experience associated with the teacher's own curriculum area, there was a better chance of making progress in the classroom. The observations and interviews provide support for subject-focused advice; teachers who demonstrate mastery of key aspects of culturally responsive pedagogies in their subject areas could play an important teacher leadership role in differentiated professional development to support their peers.

Conclusion

A total of 318 valid systematic classroom observations in 22 project schools, 98 comparison observations in 10 non-project schools, and interviews with more than 165 teaching staff demonstrated that the Te Kotahitanga professional development program did change teacher practice. While the limitations of the evaluation did not allow teacher change to be measured over time, it was possible for teachers to articulate the impact of the professional development on their practice. The analysis of in-class observations indicated that nearly 3 out of 4 teachers in project schools evidenced either moderate or high implementation of the Effective Teacher Profile (ETP). A further set of observations in non-project schools demonstrated that Te Kotahitanga halved the proportion of low implementers and increased the proportion of high implementers many times over, demonstrating significant impact of the professional development on teacher classroom practice.

This chapter focused on three clear themes of change evident in the data: teacher positioning, co-construction and student-focused classrooms; teachers caring for students as culturally located individuals: and teachers' monitoring and assessment. The observation data revealed that the type of classroom activity altered depending on the teacher's level of ETP implementation. Teachers who were high implementers adopted agency for learning as they organized instruction for active participation, ensured that content was relevant and in some cases included Māori cultural knowledge, and communicated high expectations to students.

While most teachers in the evaluation were implementing the Effective Teaching Profile, the fact that as many as 1 in 4 teachers were not would suggest that a professional development program that focuses on culturally relevant pedagogy alone may not be sufficient. Several challenges may inhibit the ability of some teachers to make change in the classroom, such as misconceptions or beliefs regarding the program and a lack of classroom management and other teaching skills. It appears that while Te Kotahitanga as a professional development program needs to adapt to meet the needs of some teachers starting at different places, with different subject needs, a faction of teachers will require additional support to address competency issues, perhaps outside the scope of the program.

· 7 ·

THE IMPACT OF CULTURALLY RESPONSIVE PEDAGOGIES ON STUDENTS AND FAMILIES

Wally Penetito, Rawiri Hindle, Anne Hynds, Catherine Savage, and Larissa Kus, Victoria University

Introduction

How well students perform in school classrooms is of paramount importance first of all to the students themselves, then to their teachers and third to the parents or caregivers of the students. How each of these parties makes judgments about the worth or otherwise of student performance is a matter of debate. If parents and caregivers perceive their family members are happy to go to school each day and motivated to learn what the school has to offer, they will generally be content and satisfied that the school and its teachers are doing their job (Bishop & Berryman, 2006, ch. 4). Teachers likewise will feel satisfied they are doing what they have been trained to do using the same two criteria of student happiness in being present and motivation to learn. As professionals they will more than likely expect that student attendance is more than just being present as some form of routine, regulation or ritual, but that students want to be there; it is an excited or at least energized presence rather than one that has a compulsory aspect to it. What drives teachers more than anything else are students who are there because they want to learn, they want to acquire knowledge, and they want to be part of the educative process (Bishop in Timperley et al., 2007, p. xvii). The judgments that students make about the conditions for their own school performance are far more complex than those made by their parents or their teachers. Schools exist for them; they have a tacit appreciation of this. Laws and regulations are written to ensure that being at school for designated periods of time is mandatory. They learn this requirement from their parents the first time they feign illness rather than having to sit 'the test'. Moving from one school to another, students discover how buildings and associated constructions have a familiarity about them and that even the architecture serves some kind of regulatory requirement where predictability of structure is designed with them in mind. More than anything else they quickly come to understand that teachers teach to an officially sanctioned curriculum, and that teachers exercise appropriate pedagogies depending on the student stage of learning, the subject of the curriculum, and the best practice for implementing that curriculum according to current research.

Students come 'to know' that these things are what schools are about and what school life means. Students who accept most of what schools are about are rewarded, those who resist certain elements of school life, like the routines and structures, are cajoled into accepting them as being in their best interests. Those who are confounded by the sheer complexity of school life are left to roam the corridors like bewildered rabbits. Those who for reasons beyond their comprehension become detached and eventually reject what the school stands for become subjects of research. The classical description of classroom life discussed by Jackson (1968) is a forerunner of this type of analysis. This is not the full range of student identities but they debatably are the most common. It is critical for our understanding as teachers or parents and certainly students that each of these four 'ideal types' is capable of being a successful learner in the school environment, that is, they each have the 'cultural intelligence' to "analyse their experiences of being excluded" where this occurs "and propose ways to reverse their situation" (Oliver, de Botton, Soler, & Merrill, 2011, p. 267). It is also critical to keep in mind that as well as these evolving 'institutional biographies,' all students arrive at schools with well-developed self-perceptions of their own learning abilities, of the rules of the game of life and living and of strategies for negotiating the various terrain.

Given the prior conditions outlined, becoming a successful part of school life might sound like quite a tall order for many students. In the New Zealand context this is true of the indigenous group self-defined as Māori. This book is based on a professional development initiative, Te Kotahitanga, designed and implemented to bring about educational success for Māori students beginning in their first two years of mainstream secondary schooling, namely, years

9 and 10. This chapter will elicit data from our evaluation of Te Kotahitanga to ascertain its impact on Māori students and their achievement. Within mainstream schooling the question as to whether Māori students can succeed in a system without having to sacrifice their unique Māori identities is an important discussion that arises out of the data.

Following this discussion is the question of impact of Te Kotahitanga on the families or whānau of students. Culturally responsive pedagogies do impact on both students and their parents. Teachers who are aware of their own cultural configurations and acquire the humility to learn from the Māori students and their parents will, as a consequence of the Te Kotahitanga professional develop- ment program, likely become culturally responsive pedagogues. It can be claimed all that Māori students have ever needed through schooling was the opportunity for equal access to their own cultural milieu. With that access they can then learn to succeed as Māori or not. This last point is briefly discussed in the concluding section of this chapter. Historically they have not had that opportunity because neither the curriculum nor the teaching practice significantly responded to their cultural backgrounds but instead imposed the dominant group's knowledge, stan- dards, values, expectations and attitudes on both curriculum and pedagogy.

Learning and Belonging as Māori

In order to estimate the impact of Te Kotahitanga on students' experiences in schools, we briefly summarize highlights of student narratives from *Culture Speaks* (Bishop & Berryman, 2006), which can serve as a baseline for judging the extent to which Māori students' experiences in school changed as a result of their teachers' participation in the Te Kotahitanga program. Recall from Chapter 2 that these narratives were drawn from academically engaged and non-engaged Māori students in five secondary schools prior to the design of the Te Kotahitanga project. As such, they offer a window into what Māori students' experiences are like in mainstream secondary schools without the project.

Being Māori in mainstream schools without Te Kotahitanga

According to Bishop and Berryman (2006), the majority of Māori students who were interviewed emphasized that they wanted to succeed in school, but found the experience of trying to succeed to be painful mainly because of conflicts with teachers and low expectations for Māori student learning that resulted in students not getting the help they needed. For example:

> Well, most of the teachers—they tell Pākehā kids that their work is not up to standard, and they'll need to see their parents if it doesn't improve. They don't say that to us! It's like they don't expect our whānau to get us going. (p. 33)

When students described wanting to learn 'as Māori', they talked about wanting teachers to pronounce their names correctly, recognize that they have knowledge of things Māori, and show willingness to learn from the students. For example, one student said:

> We do a unit on respecting others' cultures. Some teachers who aren't Māori try to tell us what Māori do about things like a tangi (funeral). It's crap! I'm a Māori. They should ask me about Māori things. I could tell them about why we do things in a certain way. I've got the goods on this, but they never ask me. I'm a dumb Māori I suppose. Yet they asked the Asian girl about her culture. They never ask us about ours. (p. 76)

Students also wanted teachers to recognize that Māori students have learning strategies that work for them, rather than assuming that they do not:

> Most of the teachers don't understand how we really want to learn, how we can learn. They don't know about us and they're too strict. (p. 8)

The remark above led to a discussion about what it means to be strict. Students said that most teachers were strict about the wrong things, centering on minor behavior infractions rather than academic learning. And in so doing, they made Māori students feel singled out unfairly; for example:

> Teachers usually know who smokes, and being Māori means you get hunted more. If you are on the field, and there's a bunch of Māori and a bunch of Pākehā, they'll usually go to the Māori. (p. 80)

Students said that what they wanted most when they went to school was relationships with teachers that would translate into quality teaching, without teachers expecting the students to be someone other than who they are.

> They have gotta want to be with us, and they've gotta be enthusiastic, and they've gotta be not boring, and they've gotta talk with us about stuff in the lesson—like what we already know or how we might have a go at things. (p. 34)

Ask us about our names. Find out about famous Māori from around here. . . . We might tell the teacher or we might not, but at least they're interested in us when they ask. (p. 78)

Students also described their preference for group work in the classroom, and for being asked to give input into class work. For example, one student described at some length a unit that students learned from and enjoyed. The main feature of the unit was that the students helped to plan it: "We worked as a team and we made decisions" (p. 109).

Although students described teachers who respected them and taught them well, the dominant theme of their description of school was of negative and painful experiences.

Learning as Māori in Te Kotahitanga schools

Across the 22 schools, we interviewed 214 Māori students in 39 focus groups, who were enrolled in Years 10–13. We asked students how they felt about school, their learning, learning as Māori and other issues of cultural identity, and aspects of Te Kotahitanga. We highlighted the question regarding whether 'being Māori' looked different in school compared to outside of school in order to find out how Māori identity was represented in and out of school as well as whether students felt that this identity was welcomed in the classroom. Each focus group was facilitated by two researchers, at least one of whom was Māori.

While students were able to describe teachers who did not respect them or teach them well, these interviews were overwhelmingly positive about the kinds of teacher-student relationships and classroom teaching they were experiencing. Students were able to articulate changes that they had experienced and seen in the teachers since the beginning of the Te Kotahitanga program. A particular noted change was teachers who had moved from the traditional chalk and talk method to more interactive approaches:

My teacher Mr. B he was like, just writing hard out, writing hard out and we were like, he'd write it down and it's like all of a sudden he starts being real cool. Laid back and started interacting with us . . . over a period of time he's become more cool . . . more interactive with the students. (Māori student)

Students were able to identify and describe teaching methods they preferred, including group arrangements for learning, positive social relationships in the classroom, peer teaching activities, self-assessment and added resources such as colored cards and activity cards. Several student groups specifically stated that they had seen some teachers changing their teaching at school:

> It's because she is fun, she makes it interactive and it's like you learn more, and we do book work but not all the time. She's on our level, and it's as though she is one of us, not like a teacher, she's like real cool and will get in there with you. Not like other teachers, here's book work go and do it, she'll give us mean activities to do, like fun and you can work with your whole class instead of just like this . . . like our whole classroom does it together and then we can do it in groups, it's real cool, and she does positive learning tips at the start, you're not allowed to be negative, no put-downs . . . commitment and respect, it's real cool.

Māori students were also clearly aware of and sensitive to teacher expectations, and they appreciated the efforts of teachers who drove them to achieve at their personal best at school:

> Like some teachers will push you to what, the level you should be at and some will push you to go further and it's better because like, yeah they make you feel like a better person.

The Māori students appreciated the efforts their teachers were making that demonstrated valuing student knowledge and that communicated respect for students' ideas and prior knowledge. Students spoke positively about teachers who made an effort to get to know them, helped them in class, made them 'use their brains' and monitored their progress while also emphasizing respect and caring:

> If you tell them what you want to learn, they'll incorporate it, let you choose what you want to learn.

> They respect us as Māoris.

> She brings us into the conversation, she asks questions like why they came and how they came, when I first came and why I am doing this—I don't know about the migration story, I've learnt stuff about Māori migration that I didn't know.

When we asked the students what it meant to 'be Māori' at school, most were able to discuss what this meant to them. For example:

> To me, it means expressing the culture of being a Māori and not being afraid or shy to show it.

I'm tangata whenua (person of this land), I can carry my Māori culture to the next generation.

Students were also able to discuss ways in which schools and teachers did or did not enable them to be Māori at school:

> Nothing makes me personally feel like I shouldn't be Māori, because that's just who I am and they can't change that. Some things like with the teachers it feels like they're targeting us and it's like oh, is it because I'm Māori? Or is it because of the people I'm hanging out with that are also Māori?

> The Māori teachers they always encourage you to take Māori and they say 'You should be involved for NCEA'. It's good because the Māori teachers they encourage you so you don't lose your culture.

In several student focus groups, students discussed how teachers attempted to speak te reo Māori in the classroom:

> Our maths teacher she always tried to speak Māori which is very cool because she like writes the date up in Māori for our class. She tried to say some instructions in Māori like what she does, so yes we found it pretty cool how some of our teachers try to [speak Māori].

> Yeah he's learning he's on the same road as us. Yes we always learn, we teach him new things and he like tries to talk to us in Māori and he says what's this or what's the Māori name for this and then says it all the time. But he's learnt heaps, like when he first came into our class he didn't know any Māori, didn't know how to say things and we just teach him now.

Students appreciated teachers who tried to understand and acknowledge the experiences of being Māori and use Māori culture and/or language in their classrooms:

> Ms C speaks to us in Māori and sometimes she says the numbers in Māori, the countdown—she comes to the marae and the wananga a lot and when we have visitors she comes and listens to the whaikorero.

> In dance and drama, on a wall there are all these Māori words. Every day she picks a different way to say Good Morning in Māori.

Students identified teachers using the Māori date and time, writing numbers, basic commands and greetings and saying students' names correctly. They saw it as positive that teachers would use Māori in the classroom, and liked to help teachers with pronunciation.

Some try to talk Māori. They ask you Māori words. I appreciate it when they do that.

Mr. B, he gets up and does a whaikorereo and tried to learn our karakia that we do.

If she's reading a story and it's got some Māori words in it she'll look to us and then be like 'Is that OK? Is that how I say it? And she includes us in everything.

Yeah we help them out, we felt really cool that they actually try and give it a go.

Several Māori students also recognized teachers' efforts to include more Māori concepts in lessons:

The teachers always tell us like how Māori were the first people to come to NZ from Hawaiiki.

In Science, (the teacher) told us about the water cycle, when it rains it's Rangi, he was crying for Papatuanuku.

Science, we're learning about living things—she did like all these flax things and had to find all the Māori names and things.

In art, we are doing a project that involves all different cultures, Māori, Pacific Island. She gets involves with Māori stuff. For example, we did an ink print that used an organic shape, and involved Māori and Pacific Island patterns. Even though it was art, we learned protocol, like how to cut and work with flax.

Summary

Across the 22 schools, the way Māori students described their experiences in school, relationships with teachers, and expression of their cultural identity in school was markedly different from the narratives Bishop and Berryman (2006) reported in the 5 mainstream secondary schools prior to the development of Te Kotahitanga. Although students we interviewed were able to identify teachers who did not show interest in them or teach them well, and although several students described examples of racism in their schools, the great majority of students' comments affirmed the students' appreciation for efforts their teachers were making to get to know them, learn something of Māori culture and language, and make the learning experience work for students. Even though teachers' knowledge of Māori culture and language was largely rudimentary, the fact that many teachers were willing to learn from their students rather than penalizing Māori students based on inaccurate assumptions about them mattered very much to the students.

Impact on Student Achievement

The ultimate goal of Te Kotahitanga is not just to change teacher behavior, but to change it toward enhancing Māori student educational success. Our independent evaluation included an analysis of changes in student achievement as a function of implementation of the model. One complication for investigating this relationship is that in New Zealand, while Te Kotahitanga is focused on Years 9–10, no systematic or system-wide achievement assessments are carried out with all students during these school years. Individual schools may employ a standardized assessment of mathematics, science, and other subject areas for which such tests might be available, but this is entirely a school matter. In contrast, assessments in Years 11–13 for New Zealand's standards-based National Certificate of Educational Achievement (NCEA) provide detailed data on student performance across subjects, including both classroom assessments and final examinations that are 'moderated' (i.e., checked independently on a random basis by subject experts). These assessment results are thus comparable nationally across schools and are recorded and were available to us for all students at all schools.

Year 9–10 student achievement outcomes

The first teacher cohort received their first full year of training in 2004, so they can be considered to be engaged in full implementation of the model in 2005. The second teacher cohort received their first full year of training in 2005, so they can be considered to be engaged in full implementation of the model in 2006. By 2006, then, one might expect evidence of enhanced student achievement for Year 9 and Year 10 students. Ideally, grades in the different subjects students take would be reported and could be analyzed for those years. While teachers in New Zealand do not record grades on any formal record before Year 11, schools do have access to several available standardized tests in a few core subject areas such as numeracy/mathematics, science and literacy, and these are used at some schools. To measure Year 9 and Year 10 student achievement, the Te Kotahitanga project adopted one such test, the *Assessment Tool for Teaching and Learning* (asTTle), from 2005 onwards, and the project encouraged schools to use asTTle to measure literacy and numeracy outcomes. Nevertheless, project schools did not consistently use asTTle or any other achievement measure in Years 9–10, so that these data were not available across schools nor were they available for comparison schools. Thus, the independent evaluation had no source of representative assessments that could be analyzed to investigate project impact on student achievement in those years.

Longer-term student achievement outcomes: Years 11–13

While Te Kotahitanga is focused on professional development for teachers who are teaching Years 9 and 10, the majority of teachers who teach Years 9–10 classes also teach senior secondary subjects across Years 11–13. Thus, one might expect teachers to extend their understandings of culturally responsive pedagogies and effective teaching dimensions to how they approach teaching older students as well. Evidence regarding whether or not teachers generalize new learnings to teaching practice in the senior secondary school was not within the scope of the independent evaluation. Nevertheless, the students who attend Te Kotahitanga project schools for Years 9–10 could be expected to show the impact of Te Kotahitanga on their achievement later, when they move on to Years 11–13 and begin participation in the NCEA. To what extent is this kind of transfer realistic, and when might we expect it this to become evident?

As was discussed in Chapter 4, any investigation of the impact of Te Kotahitanga on long-term achievement outcomes must take implementation timelines into consideration. Any results based on outcomes in Years 11–13 must also be qualified given the absence of direct evidence that teaching and learning in the senior subjects and Years 11–13 continue to reflect Te Kotahitanga practices. Instead, teaching activities in these senior subject classes could reflect traditional practices and be driven by perceptions of the demands of the NCEA, rather than Te Kotahitanga facilitation and co-construction teams. Observation of teacher practice in senior subjects is needed to address the extent to which teachers are able to generalize their new skills in culturally responsive pedagogies to the final three years of secondary school.

In the next sections, we summarize some of the major findings for changes in student achievement–related factors across time: student retention beyond age 16, Year 11 NCEA achievement in selected subjects, Year 12 NCEA achievement overall, and the percentage of students who complete secondary school with the qualifications needed for university study. These findings are analyzed in comparison to student results at a set of matched schools using the quasi-experimental design described in Chapter 4.

Student retention

In New Zealand, as in many other countries, students are required to attend school until they are 16 years of age. Thus, remaining in school after age 16 and returning to school the following year represents an important indicator often referred to as retention. The data revealed a dramatic increase in retention across the senior secondary years in Te Kotahitanga schools. This increase suggests that a broader range of students were being retained at all schools in contrast to earlier patterns whereby lower achieving students left school without qualifications. Both Te Kotahitanga and comparison schools show this numerical increase in retention, but the increased retention of students in Year 11 is proportionately highest at Te Kotahitanga schools. For students of European descent, Year 11 numbers increased from 590 in 2005 to more than 1,000 in 2008, an increase of approximately 59%. For Māori, Year 11 numbers increased from 376 in 2005 at the Te Kotahitanga schools and 336 in the comparison schools, to 996 and 797, respectively, in 2008. At the Te Kotahitanga schools, this represented increased Māori student increase of more than 260%.

Year 11 NCEA achievement

In New Zealand, Year 11 is the first of the final 3 years of secondary school and is also the first year for which formal student grades are recorded in the different subjects. In Year 11, students are enrolled in a large number of credits (120 or more) providing opportunities to pass the 80 credit minimum required for the NCEA Level 1 certificate. However, the NCEA system is designed to be seamless, so that schools can enable students to gain each certificate by working across 2 or more years. Even though this is less desirable (and generally seen to be an adaptation for lower achieving students), a percentage of students continue to take more than one year to complete Level 1 so that partial accumulation toward 80 credits can be indicative of progress. Thus, the national database of student achievement summarized each year by the Ministry of Education includes this early indicator, expressed as the percentage of students who attain 40 or more credits in Year 11.

All Year 11 students at the Te Kotahitanga schools were performing slightly but not significantly below those at the comparison schools in 2004 in the percentage of students attaining 40 or more credits, which was rising gradually for all students. Figure 7.1 shows that by 2009, the percentage of Year 11 students attaining at least 40 credits at Te Kotahitanga schools (58.1%)

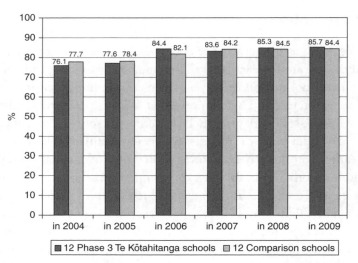

Figure 7.1 Percentage of all Year 11 students attaining 40 or more credits at NCEA Level 1 or higher, 2004–2009

had surpassed that at the comparison schools (56.6%). (These data include all students, Māori and non-Māori, as a breakdown by ethnicity was not available.) Because of the small sample size with only 12 schools in each group, these small percentage differences are not statistically significant.

While progress toward receiving a certificate in Year 11 is positive, a higher expectation would be for students to pass the 80 credit minimum required to be awarded the first NCEA Level 1 certificate. Figure 7.2 reports the percentage of all Year 9 entrants who attained NCEA Level 1 in Year 11 in each year from 2004 to 2009. Again, the baseline for the percentage of Year 9 entrants from 2002 who attained NCEA Level 1 in 2004 was lower at the Te Kotahitanga schools (38.1%) than at comparison schools (43%). By 2009, students at the Te Kotahitanga schools showed a greater gain across these years, ending with a slightly higher percentage at the project schools having gained NCEA Level 1 in 2009—58.1% versus 56.6%. That is, there was a 20% increase in student attainment of NCEA Level 1 at the project schools compared with a 13.6% increase at comparison schools.

Year 12 NCEA Achievement

Students on track to gain the three NCEA certificates in each of the final three years of secondary school would need to complete both NCEA Level 1

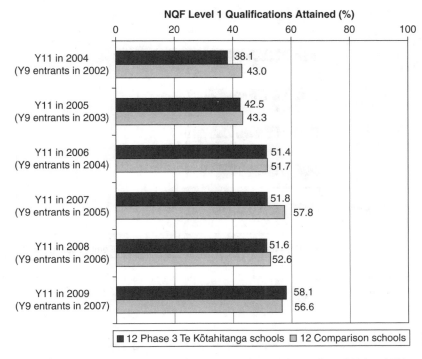

NQF Level 1 Qualifications Attained (%)

Figure 7.2 Attainment of NCEA Certificate at Level 1 in Year 11 from 2004 to 2009 as a percentage of school roll in Year 9 when each year group entered school 2002–2007.

and NCEA Level 2 certificates by the end of Year 12. Figure 7.3 shows the percentage of students across the project and comparison schools who completed NCEA Level 2 in Year 12 within three years after Year 9; these students are still on track for the possibility of attaining all three certificates before leaving school at the end of Year 13. Across all schools, this percentage increased 10% from slightly more than one-third of students in 2005 to approximately 45% by 2009. The percentage for Te Kotahitanga schools is only marginally higher than for the comparison schools, a difference that is not particularly meaningful given the slight variation from year to year as well.

School leaver qualifications

Expectations that the project will have an impact on student achievement become increasingly optimistic as time passes. Again, as discussed earlier in this chapter, we don't know if the teachers continued to use their new pedagogical

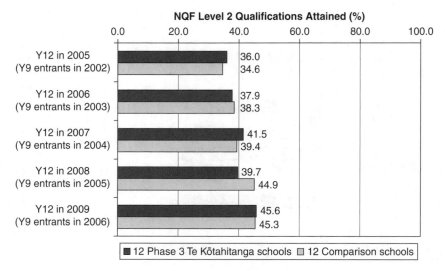

Figure 7.3 Attainment of NCEA Level 2 Certificate in Year 12 in 2005–2009 as a percentage of the school roll in Year 9 when each year group entered school 2002–2006.

skills in the senior school. Furthermore, as the students themselves progress through the senior school, the 'distance' since being in Years 9–10 becomes greater and their achievement can be affected by many factors occurring during the intervening years. Nevertheless, we examined final achievement outcomes at the end of secondary school; one reason for doing this was that there had been early concerns that the school program focus on Māori student achievement could have a differential impact on achievement for other students. Despite the potential relevance of examining these long term outcomes, however, there is one important caveat: technically, it is too early to evaluate the direct impact of Te Kotahitanga on Māori students in Year 13, as the initial student cohorts experiencing the full model had not yet completed their secondary education by 2009.

Over the longer term, the level of qualifications attained by students when they leave school—whether this is before Year 13 or after the full 13 years of schooling—is the crucial outcome. New Zealand government policy now supports that no student should leave school without at least a Year 12 qualification (Ministry of Education, 2009). Two outcomes that are crucial long term achievement outcomes are the percentage of students who: (a) leave school with only a minimum or no qualification (certificate), and (b) finish school with the required qualifications to be eligible for university entrance.

The Te Kotahitanga and comparison schools are similar with respect to the percentage of students leaving school without qualifications from 2004 to 2009: the schools in both groups mirror the national pattern of a large decrease in students leaving school without any formal qualifications—from more than 15% to about 5% of all school leavers across these six years.

Similarly, all 24 schools show improvement across the same six-year period (2004–2009) in the percentage of all Year 13 school leavers who qualify for university entrance, the increase being slightly higher for the Te Kotahitanga schools. It is not surprising that there has been an increase generally in secondary school student outcomes during this time. Te Kotahitanga is one of various initiatives supported by government to raise achievement in schools, particularly at lower decile schools such as the 24 schools in the project and the comparison sample. These school leaver data suggest ongoing improvements in educational performance in the final three years of secondary school across all schools.

A caveat: Early days for impact on student achievement

Evidence based on NCEA findings are early days even for these 12 schools, where the first student cohort to experience full implementation of Te Kotahitanga did not reach Year 11 until 2008 and had only reached Year 12 by 2009—the latest year in which student outcome achievement data were available for our analyses. Thus, any conclusive findings regarding impact of Te Kotahitanga on school leavers would require at least one more year of data, from 2010. Further, it would be inappropriate to compare results on the NCEA at the schools that began Te Kotahitanga in 2006 until at least the 2010 data are available, given that no student cohort experiencing full implementation had reached Year 11 by 2009.

Nevertheless, the analyses of evidence on student achievement in the senior secondary school revealed that the presence of Te Kotahitanga in schools was associated with greater retention into the senior high school, beyond compulsory attendance age. Students in Te Kotahitanga schools also passed more credits in the senior high school in comparison to peers at matched comparison schools, despite the possibility that increased retention may mean a higher percentage of lower achieving students were staying in school. At school completion, both sets of schools showed improvement in lower numbers of students leaving school with minimal qualifications and higher numbers of students qualifying for university entrance. Overall,

Te Kotahitanga schools showed slightly higher performance with respect to student eligibility for university entrance—suggesting that what was good for Māori students was also good for other students throughout the school.

Impact on Families

What parents and care givers know about the impact of the Te Kotahitanga program in their school and on their young people will in most cases derive from the behavior of their young people at home rather than from a direct relationship with the school and its teachers. Some will of course have a direct relationship either in a school governance role as Boards of Trustees[1] members or some other of a variety of formal fraternities common at secondary school level. One of these, the Whānau/Family Support Group, the research evaluation team took advantage of by structuring sessions with them to discuss their views about Te Kotahitanga and in particular whether they had observed changes of behavior with their young people in regard to schooling. Māori support groups have emerged in a number of schools although they are still a relatively new phenomenon. As a support group, initially established to support Māori students but with the potential to also stand alongside teachers and the school as a whole, they bring their own flavour of liaison into the relationship between schools and Māori communities. The flavour can be described as elements of Māori culture as evidenced in tikanga (custom), āhuatanga (Māori ways of doing things), and wairua (a spiritual, holistic dimension). Most of the data reported in this section is from the interviews with Whānau Support Groups.

Whānau support groups

In most cases whānau were confident about what they thought the schools were trying to do to help their children learn. Confidence was built around what they saw as formal attempts to address student achievement by focusing on improving relationships between teachers and students rather than fixating on what teachers perceived as non-compliant behavior at best and aberrant behavior at worst. Te Kotahitanga brought an expression of new confidence and a sense that secondary schools could be on the path to recognizing different sets of values than those that typically privilege knowledge over experience, differentiation over connectedness, and the individual over the collective. As an example, the Māori value of te kanohi e kitea, the face that's seen, can be read into this statement. It's important to show one's face when there is a gathering but not only when the big events occur. In Māori terms, there is greater respect for the face that is seen on a regular basis no matter what the occasion.

We have elicited some of the typical comments from whānau as evidence of the points raised under the heading of relationships with the community:

> It's like one big family, one big whānau with our children here.

> My hopes and dreams for my daughter are like any parents, what my parents gave me, and that's to feel loved and to have a whānau that they know will support them, regardless of their academic achievements. For me, I want my daughter to contribute to the community in a positive way . . . to believe in, well to stand up for what she believes in and to be a loyal friend to others, to herself, to be honest to herself, and I think that college will absolutely assist her on that pathway. The friends she makes here, I've told her, your friends at high school will be friends for life.

> It's good for both cultures to learn about each other. We're learning all the tauiwi (foreign) ways. The Pākehās need to learn some of the Māori way, so I think that a blending of two cultures would be good. It's good for our own kids too you know. Our Māori kids see that kaumatua (elders) are here and supporting them. I think more of that needs to be done. I don't think a lot of that was done in the past.

Whānau groups were generally aware of the existence of something called Te Kotahitanga that was operating in their schools. They all knew it was a program that targeted their children and had something to do with raising achievement levels but most knew little more than that. Because the program had a Māori name, most were positively disposed toward it but felt the school needed to do a lot more to inform them about what it was and how it worked.

Parental motivation generated through Te Kotahitanga

While most parents knew little of the details of the Te Kotahitanga program in their schools, what they did know was that their family members were excited and they were talking at home about their teachers more than usual and about the work they were doing at school. These were two topics rarely volunteered previously and when raised were often in negative terms. This from a teacher who works with his school's Whānau Support Group:

> If you've got anything that showcases a student's work, if you have a concert or a performance, you will get people to come to that. Getting them to be involved in goal

setting is a whole other agenda. And we continue to struggle with that, to battle with that. And I don't know the answer. I don't know the answer across the whole school community, more than just with our Māori students.

For many parents, the entry of their children into the secondary school system is like a signal that says, 'Ok. Now they're yours for the duration of the school day'. Despite what some parents might say, they seem to only want to know how their child is doing at school as this relates to achievements and/ or misbehavior. Other than that the belief seems to be 'no news is good news'. There is no doubt that Te Kotahitanga focuses on the educative process and especially in the culturally responsive pedagogy of relations and this message, probably somewhat garbled, appears to be getting through to Māori parents via their children. One effect of this 'special' interest is to question the boundary between those on the inside of groups and those on the outside:

> Staff encourage Māori Whānau to work here to be teachers. Back in 2005 [there was] only about 1 or 2 Māori teachers [but there are] more Māori teachers now [but we] still need more.

While whānau appreciated the Te Kotahitanga program, they felt that the system needed to change as well to support Māori students. Whānau acknowledged that it was difficult for the program to be successful when it was being implemented in a system that was non-Māori. This point is raised again in the conclusion to this chapter.

> I agree the principal is supportive. But in the mainstream curriculum, how much is directly about Māori history, entrepreneurs, and Māori role models? That to me is directly linked to the value of Māori in the school. It is a sad thing to hear my children say "Why do they say Māori don't attend school?" Because my kids always attend, they go to school, so it's about the messages the kids get about being Māori in the mainstream. That's why you have to look at the system, otherwise Te Kotahitanga it's a Māori concept trying to work in a non-Māori environment.

There was significant discussion in each of the whānau groups concerning whānau and their access to the school, and their own feelings of belonging-ness at the school. This was dependent on the context of each school. One school in particular had made a significant effort to employ whānau in the learning support centre and in doing so had given whānau a place within the school.

In two focus groups, whānau expressed their view that there was some way to go before whānau and school could work together. In one instance, whānau stated that past injustices needed to be addressed and healed before the program could be successful.

> We are here at the school. As I said before, things are starting to change, we are starting to see more whānau here, but as people have said there needs to be more honesty and more communication between us all—we are here to help. If the project is Te Kotahitanga then that is about unity, I am not sure we are there yet.

> I have an in-depth knowledge about the program, but communication from the school has been minimal. The program only started being implementing this year. Brilliant program if it's implemented. Many years of healing has got to take place (with the Māori community) before it can work.

In general, the whānau we interviewed made it clear that they were positive about the implementation of the Te Kotahitanga program in their school. They reported that it was still early days but in some schools whānau detected a change in the teachers and the way in which the school valued 'things Māori'. Some participants highlighted the support they had received from individuals including teachers, facilitators, and/or members of the school's senior management team. However, one particular whānau group felt that their school did not provide enough support or acknowledgement for Māori. In addition, another whānau group regarded the school as discriminatory, and that it did not communicate with parents or value parental input. The data from this school was in contrast to the other whānau groups that were generally more positive about the school and their children's progress. Whānau were adamant that to improve Māori student outcomes, schools needed to develop culturally responsive systems.

Whānau noted several different outcomes of Te Kotahitanga, and these were more likely to be outcomes that supported the student culturally including increased pride, a willingness to attend the marae (traditional Māori space) and an increasing interest in the school. Some whānau groups stated that Māori teachers were important in the school and had contributed to their students learning in positive ways. However, most whānau groups had one or two descriptions of teaching that had not changed, of teachers who didn't expect much and did not encourage their children to learn.

Whānau who were involved in the school, either as employees or on the Board of Trustees, were significantly more positive about the school, the Te Kotahitanga program and the changes that they had seen in the teachers and school.

We've got a Māori parents group and they've been kept informed about what is going on. We've not had, I guess we've not had any real active interest other than—I think people recognize and value that we are trying to do something for their children. But also it really demarcates you and therefore there is a receptiveness by particularly Māori students and Māori parents in regard to that. So I work in that role, I'm a member of the whānau support, I attend the meetings, and it's quite interesting because . . . a couple of parents, Māori parents came along to the hui and had a bit of a bash at the school. And challenged my right to be at this whānau meeting, where we were meeting with ERO [The Education Review Office]. And he said "X comes to all our meetings, he just doesn't come up—turns up to have a bit of a whinge or a moan or a poke at the school. And we'd love to have you turn up."

One school in particular had sought out whānau members to work in the school, and the whānau believe that this had a positive impact on their involvement in school, on the culture of the school and their child's schooling. Similarly another whānau group had attended the Te Kotahitanga hui with staff and were clearly able to articulate the program and the benefits as they saw them. Interestingly, this same whānau group noted the emphasis on underachievement and stated that this may send the wrong message to students about Māori achievement.

In summary, the commitment of Māori whānau and the school community to Te Kotahitanga and to Māori student achievement in the mainstream requires ongoing communication and information sharing. Present communication strategies with communities do not appear to be effective, nor are effective strategies for engaging with Māori whānau evident. Enhanced communication links would further support sustainability, particularly in periods of change in school leadership.

For whānau whom we interviewed, Te Kotahitanga was associated with major changes in the way their children approached school and their motivation to do well. Most stressed that while they themselves had never enjoyed coming to school, their children were enthusiastic about school and did not have to be persuaded or forced to attend. They valued high achievement for their children, and many emphasised whānau expectations that their young people would do better in school than the previous generation of Māori. They also valued that their children were 'able to be Māori' while learning, unlike how they themselves recalled feeling about being in school.

My dream for my child, my children, is something that I've not been able to give because I didn't learn Te Reo Māori [the Māori language], tikanga Māori [customs] all those things. I'd be so proud to see my son standing on the paepae [the space for formal ceremonial speech-making] doing the whaikōrero [the actual ceremonial speech]. Our Māori culture is not something that is easy to learn somewhere else, and if he can do it now [while at school], it's going to go with him for the rest of his life. That's my dream for him.

At a few schools, whānau were critical of the extent to which Māori culture and te reo were supported, and they felt that their children had to struggle to be both Māori and high achievers at school. There is no simple formula for institutional change.

I can see from the teachers there is rejection, it's a new program, but the problem is that we're still in the colonial system, it's not just the teachers, the system needs to change, there is work to be done, because we (the whānau) can see problems.

The commitment of Māori whānau and the school community to Te Kotahitanga and to Māori student achievement in the mainstream requires ongoing communication and information sharing. Present communication strategies with communities are tenuous, nor are effective strategies for engaging with Māori whānau evident. Enhanced communication links would further support sustainability, particularly in periods of change in school leadership. These links were not key elements in Te Kotahitanga, but future development of such linkages would enhance the model and school capacities to support achievement and other positive outcomes for Māori students. To some extent, the small sample of whānau whom we interviewed can be viewed as an indicator of less than optimal levels of involvement and communication with Māori families.

Conclusion

One of the more interesting findings that came out of the observations and interviews the research team experienced was the volume and scope of 'talk' that was generated by all those we worked with starting with teachers and students, then principals and Boards of Trustees members and finally Whānau Support Groups. People wanted to talk to us, they were almost without exception excited to talk with us about themselves, their teachers and school and their learning. "As everyday experience demonstrates," so Fillion (1983) tells us, "we do not just talk about things that interest us; we become interested in the things we talk about" (p. 705). This was clearly the case in the majority of Te Kotahitanga schools we visited. Māori students knew they were singled out for attention by their teachers but the reasons differed from the usual cases in that now teachers were asking them about their cultural understandings as Māori. "They wanted to learn something from us" as one incredulous student put it.

Historically it has been argued that in order to achieve in schools Māori students too often had to sacrifice their identities 'as Māori' (Simon & Smith, 2001). Now the Ministry of Education is pursuing a policy where Māori student achievement 'as Māori' is the ultimate goal (Ministry of Education, 2007). Whether that is doable or not, achievable or not is an empirical question with a number of fish-hooks attached. In this post-colonial, post-modernist era we are frequently reminded of the complexity of the worlds we live in. There is no more one monolithic Māori identity as there is no single Pākehā/New Zealand European identity. So how are teachers to address the question of ensuring that Māori students achieve in their classrooms and that they do that with their identities as Māori enhanced as well? From the viewpoint of Māori parents that is a worthy aim; after all teachers and schools seem to succeed with that goal for non-Māori students.

Here are three caveats as a starting point for teachers to address these concerns:

1. Teachers need to recognise the fact that there are lots of ways to be Māori;
2. Similar but not the same is that teachers must not treat all Māori students the same, i.e., they are Māori but need to be recognised as individuals in their own right; and
3. Teachers need to accept the idea that a Māori student's Māoriness makes him or her different from non-Māori and that this difference is a strength.

The one distinctive quality that Māori share through choice is a 'whaka-papa' link, a genealogical connection. Of course, a Māori person can deny those links or choose not to accept it as part of his or her identity or even to reject it as an identity marker. There is no necessary opposition in New Zealand to a person choosing to take that path. The Māori students and family members we met during our visits to schools ranged in terms of their identities as Māori across a wide continuum from at one end those who were fiercely proud of their Māori roots, spoke the Māori language as often as they could, and lived as Māori as purposefully as was possible for them to do so. At the other extreme were those Māori students who chose not to affirm, either privately or publicly, their Māori origins for whatever reasons but nevertheless were either identified by default through the school or their parents turning up at Whānau Support Group meetings as being Māori. What might seem to be a peculiar phenomenon is that more and more individuals of Māori and 'mixed Māori' backgrounds seem to be choosing to identify as Māori. Their reasons for doing so might be motivated to take advantage of various forms of asset settlements or compensations (Kukutai, 2003, p. 96) for some past injustices but this is a most unlikely incentive in the world of schooling and education.

All of these Māori identities are premised on something more than skin color. They all have something to say about levels of consciousness rather than blood quantum. In relation to young people they are all deeply influenced by the views they have heard at home and the experiences they have shared as whānau/family. If a reasonable number of views expressed by whānau paint a positive picture of the Māori world and if the experiences of Māori institutions and events have been shared on a regular basis there is an excellent chance young people will be positively pre-disposed toward affirming their Māoriness. The opposite is also true.

For this conclusion, two important points need emphasizing. The first is that we have no evidence to suggest that how a Māori student is categorized within the schooling context or even how a Māori student self-identifies makes any difference to the student's learning outcomes. That was not one of the things we set out to investigate nor was it something that arose out of the research that prompted us to ask new questions. The second point is an affirmation. There are lots of ways to be Māori and schools have no choice but to find ways to accommodate them all. The Te Kotahitanga program set out to shift the way teachers relate to and teach their Māori students, and by extension, all of their students, by learning to listen to how students self-identify and interpreting what they learn through some degree of knowledge of things Māori. Not only did we as researchers observe changes in teachers' classrooms, but also these changes were felt and commented on quite positively by students. As a result, Māori students were found to be staying in school in much higher numbers, and their achievement was beginning to improve.

If teachers could learn to treat all Māori students as true individuals, that is, true to themselves as Māori, that would be a good place to start. There has never been a shortage of teachers who thought that all that was needed was for teachers to treat Māori students as individuals, that is, like them. Therein lies the problem.

PROFESSIONAL DEVELOPMENT FOR CULTURALLY RESPONSIVE AND RELATIONSHIP-BASED PEDAGOGY

Christine E. Sleeter, California State University Monterey Bay,
Russell Bishop, University of Waikato, and Luanna Meyer, Victoria University

The Te Kotahitanga project of professional development for culturally responsive pedagogy is situated within a larger emancipatory effort to decolonize schooling for Indigenous students. Te Kotahitanga focuses on removing barriers to learning within teaching processes in mainstream classrooms—barriers that Māori students had identified in earlier research (Bishop & Berryman, 2006). It does so through a program of professional development that aims to shift the consciousness and pedagogical practices of teachers in those schools. In this concluding chapter, we reflect on promises of this approach and next steps the project is taking. We then reflect on limitations inherent in attempting to decolonize schooling through professional development. Finally, we suggest implications for generalizing lessons learned from this work to other contexts.

Promises of Professional Development for Culturally Responsive and Relationship-Based Pedagogy

Perhaps the greatest implication of this book is its documentation that it is possible to reduce learning disparities in secondary schools meaningfully through a relationship-based system of professional development in culturally responsive pedagogy. In Chapter 1, we noted the dearth of such research. Studies suggest that professional development most likely to change teaching practice is coherent and sustained over time, focuses on specific instructional strategies, involves teachers collectively rather than individually, and actively engages teachers in workshops with follow-up and peer coaching in the classroom (Garet et al., 2001; Joyce & Showers, 2002; Neufield & Roper, 2003; Snow-Runner & Lauer, 2005; Yoon et al., 2007). But despite the growing crisis of education disparities that effect minoritized students globally, we were not able to identify any published research that not only examined the impact of professional development for culturally responsive pedagogy on teacher practice, but also traced its subsequent impact on students.

This book confirms that a strong system of professional development in culturally responsive pedagogy can make a positive impact on minoritized students specifically, as well as on students as a whole. Indeed, it appears that, as teachers improve their ability to engage with and teach students they had found most challenging, their ability to teach all of their students improves. Chapter 7 showed meaningful differences on several indicators of achievement of Māori students as well as all students, favoring the Te Kotahitanga schools. In addition, we found evidence of improved self-identity alongside the more traditional measures of gains in student achievement. As the preferred goal of Māori people is for Māori to achieve *as Māori*, this latter gain in self-identity is of major significance for Māori and, by extension, other minoritized peoples everywhere.

We will comment on three features of the Te Kotahitanga professional development model that seem to matter most. First, the model maintains a vigilant and consistent focus on Māori student achievement and the wellbeing of Māori students. The professional development process begins in the local marae—in Māori space—where teachers' attention is directed toward the Māori students' narratives of experience in secondary schools. The classroom observation tool includes gathering data on the engagement of 5 Māori students during the lesson, then guiding the teacher in reflecting on their engagement and on the teacher's use of various dimensions of Māori culture in the classroom (such as pronunciation of Māori names, use of Māori protocols, use of Māori content knowledge, and so forth). The co-construction meetings focus specifically on what teachers are doing to improve Māori student learning in their classrooms. While some teachers find this consistent focus on Māori to be problematic, we view it as strength of the model because historically Māori have been the group least served by New Zealand schools. If schools are to close disparities, they must maintain a focus on how they are relating to and teaching students from the most marginalized communities. Shifting a focus to "all" students would allow educators to shift their attention toward what is familiar and comfortable.

Second, the professional development program systematizes a relationship-based way of working with and supporting teachers in their classrooms as they learn to use a new pedagogical approach. It models the relationship-based teaching-learning approach that teachers are learning to use with their own students. By experiencing a relationship-based model in which teachers learn to co-construct analysis of their own pedagogy with supportive facilitators, teachers become better at, and more comfortable with, the process of teaching and learning through co-construction. The evaluation team's observations of the feedback sessions with teachers revealed a process that was initially unfamiliar to both facilitators and teachers, but one in which both parties gradually became skilled. When talking about their enthusiasm for the professional development, teachers repeatedly commented on how much they valued talking things through with a supportive and knowledgeable facilitator. While the team did not ask teachers about parallels between the Effective Teaching Profile for the classroom, and the professional development process they experienced, these parallels were evident to the evaluation team, and had been intentionally designed as such by the Waikato planners.

In this way, the Te Kotahitanga model confirms the effectiveness of using student voice to develop an educational reform that aims to improve the educational achievement of Indigenous and other minoritized students. Beginning with the narratives of experience (Bishop & Berryman, 2006), Te Kotahitanga repositions teachers as learners, and minoritized students as teachers. It seeks to reconstruct a power imbalance between not only students and teachers, but also the Pākehā and Māori world, placing Māori students as the 'experts' who know best what works for them. But, as Cook-Sather (2006) has noted, while repositioning students as active agents in the reform of schooling is profoundly democratic, it is also profoundly difficult. Many people misunderstand the teacher-student relationship that Te Kotahitanga seeks to develop as only meaning a soft kind of care or liking for one's students. The relationship, however, is intended as a shift in power relations, and as conduit for communication that had not existed previously in most classrooms. As teachers listen to their Māori students, the intention is that they will hear students' desire to learn and to be respected, and they will learn what their students know and care about. Indeed, in classrooms of high-implementation teachers the evaluation team saw evidence of this shift in relationships working well.

Third, the model is planned to make extensive use of evidence in a variety of ways. The narratives of experience, on which the model was built, serve as a powerful tool of professional development as well as baseline evidence regarding how Māori students experience schools and being Māori in school. Published in the form of the book *Culture Speaks* (Bishop & Berryman, 2006), students' descriptions of how teachers treated them, and of their own desires for how to be treated in school, alongside teachers' negative depictions of students and their homes, quickly move many teachers past the defensiveness and resistance that is common in professional development for emancipatory pedagogies, as they see themselves and their students in these narratives. Once the project commences in a school, a system of gathering and learning to use evidence is initiated. Student achievement and retention data are analyzed as teachers and school leaders are guided in learning to use these data for instructional improvement. The facilitators' classroom observations provide a database for teachers to track their own shifts in pedagogy and relationships in the classroom, and for facilitators to use to trace shifts in pedagogy at the school level. At professional development hui, the Waikato team gathers and uses reflections that facilitators and principals write as a way of gauging what is working well and where improvements to the model need to be made. This system of data collection serves as a formative data feedback loop to the teachers, the school, and the Waikato team, to be used for ongoing growth and improvement. The system of data collection is also intended to strengthen the ability of teachers and schools to use evidence of student learning within their own schools as a tool for improving how Māori students are taught.

Te Kotahitanga Next Steps: Leadership Development

Based on what the Te Kotahitanga project leaders learned from the evaluation as well as the project's own ongoing data collection program and feedback loop, the project is currently engaged in leadership development for school reform within Te Kotahitanga schools (Bishop, O'Sullivan, & Berryman, 2010). By focusing on teacher professional development, the project as it was initially planned and evaluated attempted to reform schools using a bottom-up approach rather than a top-down approach in which school leaders are trained in whole-school reform. However, while classrooms are the most effective initial sites for educational reform (Alton-Lee, 2003; Elmore, Peterson, & McCarthey, 1996; Hattie, 1999, 2003), teachers who work in isolation are unlikely to develop and maintain to any significant extent "new teaching strategies spontaneously and on their own" (Elmore et al., 1996, p. 7). Therefore, teachers are better able to sustain change when there are "mechanisms in place at multiple levels of the system to support their efforts" (Coburn, 2003, p. 6). In other words, teachers are strengthened in their capacity to sustain change if they are supported by a broader systemic reform within the school and at national policy levels (Hattie, 1999).

Currently, as noted earlier, leadership for Te Kotahitanga's pedagogic reform is provided by in-school facilitators who support teachers through the professional development cycle of induction workshops, individual observations and feedback sessions, collaborative co-construction sessions and follow-up, and on-site shadow-coaching. However, in order to sustain the gains being made in these schools, it has been necessary to expand the reform to include leaders in other areas of the school (managerial, subject level, pastoral care), so that they can more effectively focus on the pedagogic leadership function of their roles. As a result, the project has expanded to include a means of institutionalizing a distributed leadership model within the schools in a systematic manner. In effect, this will serve as a means of implementing responsive structural or organizational reform, or the key to structural reform—leadership reform—in the schools in a formative, responsive manner. In doing so, the project is attempting to address the question of "what leaders need to know and do to support teachers in using the pedagogical practices that raise achievement and reduce disparities" (Robinson et al., 2007, p. 2). This focus on leadership is central to the notion of educational reform because, as Leithwood, Seashore Louis, Anderson, and Wahlstrom (2004) concluded from a detailed review of leadership literature, "leadership is second only to classroom instruction among all school-related factors that contribute to what students learn at school" (p. 7).

The model for leadership reform the project is using was developed in Bishop, O'Sullivan and Berryman (2010). It uses the mnemonic GPILSEO to identify those dimensions of effective leadership that are necessary to create a reformed institutional context that will allow the pedagogic reform that is Te Kotahitanga to flourish and to be sustained within its original schools and to be scaled up and sustained within further sites. GPILSEO stands for goals, pedagogy, institutions, leadership, spread, evidence, and ownership. In the GPILSEO model, effective leadership of sustainable educational reform:

- establishes and develops specific measurable goals so that progress can be shown, monitored and acted upon
- supports the development and implementation of new pedagogic relationships and interactions in the classroom
- changes the institution, its organisation and structures
- spreads the reform to include staff, parents, community, reform developers and policy makers so that a new school culture is developed and embedded
- develops the capacity of people and systems to produce and use evidence of student progress to inform change
- promotes and ensures that the ownership of the reform shifts are within the school

So as to allow leaders in all schools to operate in this fashion, it is planned that the Te Kotahitanga project will be expanded in three main ways. First will be expanding co-construction meetings to establish professional learning communities at other levels in the school beyond that of the classroom. The primary focus of these meetings will be collaborative problem-solving and direction-setting based on evidence of students/ groups of students' educational performance in relation to established goals. These meetings will provide prime opportunities for leaders to interrupt deficit explanations about Māori student achievement and seek alternative explanations in order that teachers and other leaders are able to work in an agentic manner. The first level of co-construction meetings will be at the school level where the Board of Trustees chairperson, the principal and members of the senior leadership team will use evidence of Maori student performance gathered at the school level to co-construct ways that they can support the staff to improve Maori student learning. The second level of co-construction meetings will be at the subject level, where middle-level leaders, those responsible for subject department areas in the schools, will use evidence gathered at departmental level to co-construct with other leaders at this level ways that they can support their staff to improve Māori students' learning. The third level will be to maintain those co-construction meetings currently developed at the classroom level where teachers of a common class, from a variety of subject areas, use evidence of Māori student performance in their classes, to co-construct ways that they can change their teaching practice so that Māori students can more effectively improve their learning and outcomes.

The second expansion will be to create opportunities for leaders to move from their current preoccupations with being administrative leaders to act more as instructional/pedagogic leaders. Opportunities will be provided to support them to undertake pedagogic observations and provide feedback to teachers in their respective subject areas.

The third expansion of support for leaders is for the project team to institute a means of providing mentoring to principals and senior leaders on a regular basis through workshops and in-school visits to these leaders with formal feedback on their project milestone reports, co-construction meeting minutes and orally-reported actions and activities.

In addition to these changes, there will be a clear delineation of tasks for leaders at their respective levels of responsibility so that the whole school's leadership team is working in concert towards supporting the changes that are taking place in the classrooms. For example, principals and Boards of Trustees chairs will be supported to set a vision and goals in relation to Māori achievement; change the organizational structure and policies to support pedagogic reform; spread the reform to include all concerned; ensure ownership of the reform; select new staff who will commit to the reform to change school policies and processes (such as streaming, the discipline system) that limit Māori student achievement; oversee the compatibility of assessment and reporting with school's aspirations to include parents and community in the education of their students; integrate all professional development in the school so that all of it is focused on achieving the school's goals; and ensure that funding is reprioritized so as to achieve the school's goals.

Other members of the senior management team will be supported to induct new teachers into the school culture; ensure quality data management systems are in place and working; reform the timetable to allow Te Kotahitanga pedagogic interventions to take place in a quality, sustainable manner; ensure that the discipline system works in a way that is supportive of a caring and learning classroom relationship; ensure that all professional development initiatives work in concert towards the school's goals; support teachers who are having problems coming to terms with the transformation of the school's culture; and participate in subject leaders' co-construction meetings.

Subject leaders will be supported to set Māori student achievement goals for their subject department/faculty; gather evidence of the participation and achievement of Māori students in their subject department/faculty; use this evidence to determine the implications for Māori students, for teachers in the department and for self as pedagogic leaders; act as pedagogic leaders for staff to support individual teachers' pedagogy emerging from evidence of student outcomes and from evidence of teacher observations; act as a general pedagogic leader (emerging from aggregated teacher observation data); re-prioritize funding and resourcing at appropriate levels; support the use of assessment for pedagogic purposes; participate in co-construction meetings for subject leaders; and conduct co-construction meetings for subject departments.

Scaling up educational reform has the potential to have a major impact on the disparities that exist in our society. In most cases these disparities are historical, ongoing and seemingly immutable. We are not claiming that educational reform on its own can cure historical disparities, but we are saying that educational reform can play a major part in a comprehensive approach to addressing social, economic and political disparities.

Limitations of Professional Development for Culturally Responsive and Relationship-Based Pedagogy

Addressing education disparities through professional development in culturally responsive pedagogy has limitations that are important to acknowledge. These limitations stem from what is not focused on or addressed.

Within the classroom, it became quite apparent to the evaluation team that a segment of teachers lacks adequate basic teaching skills. Across the two groups of schools—those that began the project in 2003 and those that began in 2006—almost one-fourth of teachers who participated in the professional development program remained at the low implementation level. While a few of these teachers were critical of the project itself (such as its focus on Māori students), classroom observations revealed many were struggling with basic classroom management and lesson planning. There were classrooms in which students were allowed to spend much of the time socializing; there were lessons pitched at a low level; and there were lessons in which the various activities seemed unrelated to each other and to any stated learning intention. These kinds of problems are beyond the scope of a professional development program that focuses on culturally responsive pedagogy, although it is possible that linking professional development in culturally responsive pedagogy with other professional development initiatives may help.

In addition, our observation that so many teachers in Māori-serving schools lacked basic teaching skills causes us to reflect on the equity issue of which students have access to teachers who have reasonably strong skills in organization and planning, and reasonably strong content knowledge. Around the world one commonly finds schools populated by students from marginalized communities to have disproportionate numbers of weak teachers. Structural approaches to understanding and addressing education disparities focus on equalizing distribution of resources, such as basic good teaching, or as a stronger measure, ensuring that students who are struggling most get the best teachers. Whether schools in more affluent communities of New Zealand have a higher proportion of strong teachers is unknown. But one cannot expect professional development in culturally responsive pedagogy to compensate for existing inequitable distribution of resources.

Professional development itself addresses only one layer of an extensive system of inequitable practices. Shifting pedagogical relationships in the classrooms, while critically important, leaves unaddressed many other ways in which schools still embody colonialism. Schools were established to replace the Indigenous language with English, and Indigenous cultures with Western—especially British—culture. The worldviews of most professionals working within the schools, the curriculum, and the relationships between schools and communities they serve still largely reflect the British colonial model. Schools also operate in a way that teaches an ideology legitimating the subordination of all things Indigenous, including Indigenous peoples.

Writing about colonial relations in the U.S., Tejeda, Espinoza, and Gutiérrez (2003) argue that mainstream education institutions reflect an internal neocolonialism that is produced and reproduced by the mutually reinforcing systems of colonial and capitalist domination and exploitation. These systems have organized social relations throughout the country's history. Formerly colonized peoples are still being socialized to occupy subordinate relationships; by teaching dominant worldviews and knowledge, schools teach young people to see such relationships as 'normal.' These relationships can be transformed, but to do so, Indigenous students must interrogate the past through a critical analysis of colonization, learn to critically analyze current relationships and inequitable life conditions, and redefine their identity in a way that enables claiming power and taking action. A Kaupapa Māori approach as self-determination by and for Māori people means claiming the right to determine one's own destiny, to define what that destiny will be, and to define and pursue the means of attaining it. Ultimately pursuing that right entails shifting the power to define what counts as meaningful student outcomes, and how the process of education should take place.

The most conventional way of conceptualizing student outcomes is through achievement testing. While we do not discount the importance of student academic achievement, for students who are members of historically marginalized communities, defining student outcomes only as academic achievement ignores their preparation for full participation within their own cultural communities (which requires knowing its language, history, philosophy, and cultural protocols), as well as development of a critical, decolonized identity. Many dimensions of conventional schooling become problematic as one broadens a vision for student outcomes to include preparation for bicultural participation, critical consciousness of systems of oppression, and the right to define one's own identity.

Professional development does not change the fact that schools are staffed primarily by members of the dominant society, rather than being fully bicultural—a problem discussed in Chapter 1. While the consciousness of this staff can be raised, raising consciousness of a teaching staff composed primarily of members of the dominant society does not substitute for building a bicultural teaching staff. It is possible that school leaders might be encouraged to hire a more bicultural staff than they have at present. School curricula, while they may incorporate bits of knowledge from historically marginalized communities, are still rooted in paradigms and worldviews of the dominant society. Systems to assess student learning are based primarily on mastery of Western and particularly British knowledge.

Further, since the formal training of teachers and school management is assumed to give professional educators the expertise that schools need, school leaders and teachers will need guidance on forming collaborative relationships with their local Māori communities and honoring perspectives and knowledge from within those communities that differs from perspectives of school professionals. Indeed, as noted in Chapter 7, several whānau who participated in focus groups saw this lack of communication and collaboration as a problem. It is this deeper set of institutionalized power relations that ultimately must be confronted if schools are to become decolonized.

Generalizing Lessons Learned to Other Contexts

Some years ago, David Berliner (2002) subtitled his comment on educational research as "The hardest science of all." He critiqued apparent expectations that rigorous methods of scientific experimentation used in the so-called hard sciences can be readily applied to investigate the effectiveness of an educational intervention, where variables are complex and context is everything:

> We do our science under conditions that physical scientists find intolerable. We face particular problems and must deal with local conditions that limit generalizations and theory building—problems that are different from those faced by the easier-to-do sciences. . . . Compared to designing bridges and circuits or splitting either atoms or genes, the science to help change schools and classrooms is harder to do because context cannot be controlled. (pp. 18–19)

Context is critical because educational settings are replete with interacting factors that influence one another at multiple levels and different times. Teaching behaviors interact with student characteristics, including motivation, past achievement, interest in the subject, attendance behaviors, and demographic variables such as socioeconomic status and cultural identity. In turn, student behavior interacts with teacher characteristics such as subject matter mastery, conceptions of learning, approaches to assessment, and demographic variables such as socioeconomic status and cultural identity. Then too there are the influences of curricula, school policies, school leadership styles, peers, families, the cultural identity of schools, and the relative wealth or poverty of the surrounding school communities. Thus, it should probably not surprise us that the research supporting the effectiveness of teacher professional development is actually quite limited with respect to having an impact on student outcomes. As discussed in Chapters 1 and 4 of this book, the link between teacher professional development and student achievement outcomes is extremely complex—for all of the reasons Berliner mentions.

The evaluation of Te Kotahitanga does, nevertheless, provide support for its effectiveness in not only promoting teacher change but certain positive outcomes for students as well. In their major review of connections between teacher professional development and student achievement, Guskey and Yoon (2009) report that only 9 studies met acceptable research design standards—none of which were at secondary level or addressed culturally responsive pedagogies. It would appear, then, that the Te Kotahitanga program and the supporting evidence reported in this book make a significant contribution to the literature in teacher education, secondary education, and culturally responsive practices. The program and its potential impact on teachers, schools, and students should be of interest internationally.

Validity of Te Kotahitanga

The scarcity of evidence about effective teacher professional development—particularly at secondary level and focused on culturally responsive practices—makes it important to consider whether this work from New Zealand has validity for use in educational systems and for teacher education activities in other countries and contexts. Validity refers to the extent to which one can support the truth and credibility of conclusions, inferences, and interpretations attributed to the program or intervention (Campbell & Stanley, 1963). Creswell (2009) describes various strategies that can be used to support the validity of interpretations and conclusions regarding effectiveness. These include the following that were included in Te Kotahitanga and its evaluation:

- Triangulation, whereby evidence is sourced from multi-method and a range of sources and participants across multiple schools and communities
- Rich description, whereby detailed stories are told that enable others to review processes, findings, and contextual factors for themselves
- Positive and negative findings, whereby the evidence presented include findings affirming the effectiveness of TeKotahitanga as well as information that is discrepant and suggests areas for additional improvement and/or relevant to adoption in other contexts
- Prolonged time, whereby the program was implemented in two distinct waves—hence testing that effects weren't simply time-bound—and the evaluation data gathered over a two-year period
- Peer de-briefing, involving additional reflections on interpretations of and conclusions drawn about evaluation findings from an external advisory group and expert reviewer to ensure resonance with practitioners and policy makers and not just the program developers and evaluation researchers

A program has internal validity if one can confidently assert—based on evidence—that intended outcomes are the result of implementing the intervention, and that the same or similar outcomes would not occur without the intervention. Internal validity of Te Kotahitanga as an effective program requires evidence that it was Te Kotahitanga that led to positive outcomes. Was something else happening in New Zealand schools that was actually responsible for positive outcomes, rather than Te Kotahitanga? Chapters 6 and 7 describe outcomes that participants clearly attributed to Te Kotahitanga, and comparison data on student achievement in Chapter 7 incorporates matched comparisons to offer further support for internal validity—that it was the program responsible for these changes rather than other factors.

Another key aspect of internal validity is the extent to which program design and outcomes are concordant with existing knowledge. The major teacher professional development components of Te Kotahitanga are consistent with those reported by Yoon et al. (2007) as characteristic of effective approaches, including dedicated teacher workshops, the involvement of outside experts, more than 30 contact hours of professional development activities, and significant structured and sustained follow-up program support activities at schools for teachers.

Consistency in implementation of the model is a key factor to support internal validity. Te Kotahitanga was not necessarily adapted for specific school or disciplinary contexts, but was implemented fairly consistently across teachers, subjects, year levels, and schools. This same consistency has different implications for external validity. External validity refers to whether or not an educational reform or new program would result in similar outcomes if adopted elsewhere, in another context. Consistency in implementation under a certain set of conditions or circumstances means that reported outcomes or findings may only apply to other contexts where those same conditions or circumstances exist. It's possible that the same intervention will be effective even in different contexts, but only a replication of results across variations in places, people, and procedures would establish external validity—the generalizability of Te Kotahitanga to other educational contexts. This issue has actually been a challenging one for educational research in particular; researchers have had to balance the demands of tight experimental control in order to assert internal validity. Consequently, an innovation or intervention reported as having been validated in the published literature may have worked under tightly controlled conditions not at all like the real world. Steckler and McLeroy (2008) call this an "inverse relationship between internal and external validity" (p. 9). Practitioners reading about an experimental intervention in a professional journal may be unable to determine if the intervention would be effective or even workable in their own setting (Meyer & Evans, 1993). Evidence that the program can be adapted for real-world educational settings is often a later stage in educational research, potentially leaving practitioners in the lurch. One of the major advantages of Te Kotahitanga is precisely that it has been implemented and evaluated on a large scale, in real-world schools, with the full range of typical teachers, and in a state-supported educational system without requiring extraordinary (often unaffordable) resources.

Generalizability of Te Kotahitanga

In the New Zealand context, the developers of Te Kotahitanga can assert both internal and external validity. Once a program has been shown to be effective in generating the desired outcomes (internal validity), practitioners will want to know that it can be adopted or adapted for their own circumstances and conditions—issues related to external validity. The fact that the program was implemented in two different phases (2003 versus 2006 start dates) across a large number of typical secondary schools supports the external validity of Te Kotahitanga—that it can be implemented anticipating similar positive outcomes across different people, schools that serve Māori students, and regions of the country. There were selection factors in identifying the first wave of school participants and, to a lesser extent, the second wave as well. However, the large number of schools involved makes it unlikely that other schools would differ in ways that would bias outcomes in those schools, at least within the New Zealand educational context. Thus, a certain amount of confidence is warranted that this program can be widely adopted in mainstream New Zealand secondary schools wherever Indigenous Māori students attend school alongside peers from the dominant Anglo-origin culture and immigrant cultural groups from throughout the world.

Would the Te Kotahitanga approach work in other educational systems and in other countries? The fact that Te Kotahitanga was developed for New Zealand secondary schools and for a specific bicultural context, based initially in narratives about Māori student achievement, is an issue requiring further investigation prior to exporting Te Kotahitanga to other national contexts in particular. The New Zealand secondary school system shares many features with secondary schools in other "Western" countries (e.g., the USA, Britain, Australia, Canada) or regions influenced by British educational traditions (e.g., Hong Kong, India and various nations in Africa). The New Zealand demographic whereby the Indigenous population is a minority in mainstream schools reflecting a dominant, non-Indigenous culture as a result of colonial histories is also not unlike that in many nations such as Native American students in U.S. schools, First Nation students in Canadian schools, and Aboriginal students in Australian schools. Castagno and Brayboy (2008) reference the international literature on culturally responsive practices, and their review suggests that the issues relating to marginalization of Indigenous students in mainstream schools are similar across contexts. Logically, one could assert that the situations are parallel wherever an Indigenous population has been colonized and the educational system reflects the colonial power—not the Indigenous population. Challenges related to racism and culturally responsive pedagogies are also relevant to other, non-Indigenous populations also subjugated in mainstream schools, such as African Americans in the U.S. or immigrants from various parts of the world in the U.S., Britain, Australia, and so on.

The detailed program description and measurement of effectiveness included in this book and other materials for Te Kotahitanga should make it possible for educators in other contexts to adopt and adapt Te Kotahitanga teacher professional development approaches towards enhancing student achievement in their schools. Even though Te Kotahitanga was developed and validated in a New Zealand educational context, its focus on teacher professional development to enhance educational outcomes for Indigenous students in mainstream secondary schools should be relevant to challenges and priorities in other nations and contexts where there is contrast between the cultural identity of the schools and its students. The fact that key features associated with effective professional development are components of Te Kotahitanga also offers support for its generalizability to other contexts. A different context will, however, present different challenges and different opportunities, requiring systematic replication to incorporate appropriate adaptations to the model based on local circumstances, conditions, and people. For example, rather than operationalizing culturally responsive pedagogy based on Māori student narratives, one would need to use narratives of students in one's own context.

What has clearly been demonstrated is that Te Kotahitanga can work in typical secondary schools with support to implement and sustain key program components across a two- to four-year period of time. Other educational systems and individual schools can utilize the information in this book to adapt Te Kotahitanga approaches for their own circumstances, conditions, and people, evaluating effectiveness by examining the impact on schools, teachers, and the students themselves.

NOTES

1. The Quest for Social Justice in the Education of Minoritized Students

1. Māori are the Indigenous peoples of New Zealand; the term "Pakeha" refers to descendents of the European colonizers of New Zealand.

2. Te Kotahitanga: Kaupapa Māori in Mainstream Classrooms

1. The Treaty of Waitangi, which was signed in 1840 between representatives of the British Crown and various Māori chiefs, is commonly regarded as the founding document of New Zealand, and the basis of power sharing between Māori and all others who are part of the nation.

5. Professional Development from Teacher and Facilitator Perspectives

1. Regional facilitators were experienced in-school facilitators who were then hired to mentor facilitators at several schools within a region.

7. The Impact of Culturally Responsive Pedagogies on Students and Families

1. Boards of Trustees are the governance structures for the compulsory sector within all New Zealand schools. They came into existence in 1988 as a result of the prior recommendation of the Taskforce to Review Education Administration, *Administering for Excellence* (Picot Report) (Wellington, 1988) and subsequent government policy, Ministry of Education, *Tomorrow's Schools* (Wellington, 1988). Representatives of the school and its community are elected every three years and are charged with the legal responsibility of ensuring the school operates in accordance with its obligations under the Education Amendment Act 1989.

REFERENCES

Alton-Lee, A. (2003). *Quality teaching for diverse students in schooling: Best evidence synthesis.* Wellington, New Zealand: Ministry of Education.

Altschul, I., Oyserman, D., & Bybee, D. (2006). Racial-ethnic identity in mid-adolescence: Content and change as predictors of academic achievement. *Child Development, 77*(5), 1155–1169.

Altschul, I., Oyserman, D., & Bybee, D. (2008). Racial-ethnic self-schemas and segmented assimilation: Identity and the academic achievement of Hispanic youth. *Social Psychology Quarterly, 71*(3), 302–320.

Ansalone, G. (2003). Poverty, tracking, and the social construction of failure: International perspectives on tracking. *Journal of Children and Poverty, 9*, 3–20.

Anyon, J. (1980). Social class and the hidden curriculum. *Journal of Education, 162*, 67–92.

Anyon, J. (2005). *Radical possibilities.* New York: Routledge.

Applebee, A. (1996). *Curriculum, as conversation.* Chicago: University of Chicago Press.

Aud, S., Fox, M. A., & Kewal Ramani, A. (2010). *Status and trends in the education of racial and ethnic minorities.* National Center for Education Statistics. Retrieved February 14, 2011, from http://nces.ed.gov/pubs2010/2010015/index.asp

Barton, P. E., & Coley, R. J. (2009). *Parsing the achievement gap.* Princeton, NJ: Educational Testing Service.

Baskerville, D. (2011). Developing cohesion and building positive relationships through storytelling in a culturally diverse New Zealand classroom. *Teaching and Teacher Education, 27*, 107–115.

Beane, J. (1997). *Curriculum integration: Designing the core of democratic education*. New York: Teachers College Press.

Berliner, D. C. (2002). Educational research: The hardest science of all. *Educational Researcher*, *31*(8), 18–20.

Berliner, D. (2006). Our impoverished view of educational reform. *Teachers College Record*, *108*(6), 949–995.

Berryman, M., Glynn, T., Togo, T., & McDonald, S. (2004). *Akorangawhakarei: Enhancing effective practices in special education, findings from four kurarumaki*. Report to Ministry of Education, Group Special Education. Wellington, New Zealand: Ministry of Education.

Billings, E. S., Martin-Beltran, M., & Hernandez, A. (2010). Beyond English development: Bilingual approaches to teaching immigrant students and English language learners. *Yearbook of the National Society for the Study of Education*, *109*(2), 384–413.

Bishop, R. (1994). Initiating empowering research. *New Zealand Journal of Educational Studies*, *29*(1), 1–14.

Bishop, R. (1996). *Collaborative research stories: Whakawhanaungatanga*. Palmerston North, New Zealand: Dunmore Press.

Bishop, R. (1997). Interviewing as collaborative storying. *Education Research and Perspectives*, *24*(1), 28–47.

Bishop, R. (2003). Changing power relations in education: Kaupapa Maori messages for 'mainstream' education in Aotearoa/New Zealand. *Comparative Education*, *39*(2), 221–238.

Bishop, R. (2005). Freeing ourselves from neocolonial domination in research: A Kaupapa Maori approach to creating knowledge. In N. Denzin & Y. Lincoln (Eds.), *The Sage handbook of qualitative research* (3d ed.) (pp. 109–138). Thousand Oaks, CA: Sage.

Bishop, R. (2008). Māori education. In H. Timperley, A. Wilson, H. Barrar, & I. Fung (Eds.), *Teacher professional learning development–Best Evidence Synthesis [BES]* (pp. xvi–xix). Wellington: New Zealand Ministry of Education,

Bishop, R., & Berryman, M. (2006). *Culture speaks: Cultural relationships and classroom learning*. Wellington, New Zealand: Huia Press.

Bishop, R., Berryman, M., Cavanagh, T., & Lamont, R. (2007). The Te Kotahitanga Observation Tool: Development, use, reliability and validity. Paper presented at NZARE, Christchurch, New Zealand.

Bishop, R., Berryman, M., Cavanagh, T., & Teddy, L. (2009). Te Kotahitanga: Addressing educational disparities facing Māori students in New Zealand. *Teaching and Teacher Education*, *25*, 734–742.

Bishop, R., Berryman, M., Powell, A., & Teddy, L. (2007). *Te Kotahitanga: Improving the educational achievement of Māori students in mainstream education Phase 2: Towards a whole school approach*. Final report to Ministry of Education. Wellington, New Zealand: Ministry of Education.

Bishop, R., Berryman, M., & Richardson, C. (2001). *Te Toi Huarewa*. Report to the Ministry of Education. Wellington, New Zealand: Ministry of Education.

Bishop, R., Berryman, M., Tiakiwai, S., & Richardson, C. (2003). *Te Kotahitanga: The experiences of Year 9 and 10 Māori students in mainstream classrooms*. Report to the Ministry of Education. Wellington, New Zealand: Ministry of Education.

Bishop, R., & Glynn, T. (1999). *Culture counts: Changing power relations in education*. Palmerston North, New Zealand: Dunmore Press.

Bishop, R., O'Sullivan, D., & Berryman, M. (2010). *Scaling up education reform: Addressing the politics of disparity.* Wellington: NZCER Press.

Bomer, R., Dworin, J. E., May, L., & Semingson, P. (2009). What's wrong with a deficit perspective? *Teachers College Record,* Date Published: June 03, 2009. Retrieved February 14, 2011, from http://www.tcrecord.org ID Number: 15648.

Borman, G. D. (2005). National efforts to bring reform to scale in high-poverty schools: Outcomes and implications. *Review of Research in Education, 29,* 1–28.

Brayboy, B. M. J. (2005). Toward a tribal critical race theory in education. *The Urban Review, 37*(5), 425–446.

Brayboy, B. M. J., & Castagno, A. E. (2009). Self-determination through self-education: Culturally responsive schooling for Indigenous students in the U.S.A. *Teaching Education, 20*(1), 31–53.

Bronfenbrenner, U. (1979). *The ecology of human development.* Cambridge, MA: Harvard University Press.

Bruner, J. (1996). *The culture of education.* Cambridge, MA: Harvard University Press.

Burr, V. (1995). *An introduction to social constructionism.* London: Routledge.

Cammarota, J., & Romero, A. (2009). The Social Justice Education Project: A critically compassionate intellectualism for Chicana/o students. In W. Ayers, T. Quinn, & D. Stovall (Eds.), *Handbook for social justice education* (pp. 465–476). New York: Routledge.

Campbell, D. & Stanley, J. (1963). *Experimental and quasi-experimental designs for research.* Chicago: Rand-McNally.

Carter, D. (2008). Achievement as resistance: Development of a critical race achievement ideology among Black achievers. *Harvard Educational Review, 78*(3), 466–497.

Castagno, A.E., & Brayboy, B.M.J. (2008). Culturally responsive schooling for Indigenous youth: A review of the literature. *Review of Educational Research, 78*(4), 941–993.

Cazden, C. B. (1989). Richmond Road: A multilingual/multicultural primary school in Auckland, New Zealand. *Language and Education, 3,* 143–166.

Chavous, T., Hilkene, D., Schmeelk-Cone, K., Caldwell, C. H., Kohn-Wood, L., & Zimmerman, M. A. (2003). Racial identity and academic attainment among African American adolescents. *Child Development, 74*(4), 1076–1090.

Cherubini, L., Hodson, J., Manley-Casimir, M., & Muir, C. (2010). "Closing the gap" at the peril of widening the void: Implications of the Ontario Ministry of Education policy for Aboriginal education. *Canadian Journal of Education, 33*(2), 329–355.

Coburn, C. (2003). Rethinking scale: Moving beyond numbers to deep and lasting change. *Educational Researcher, 32*(6), 3–12.

Connor, M. H., & Boskin, J. (2001). Overrepresentation of bilingual and poor children in special education classes. *Journal of Children and Poverty, 7,* 23–32.

Cook-Sather, A. (2002). Authorizing students' perspectives: Towards trust, dialogue, and change in education. *Education Researcher, 31*(4), 3–14.

Cook-Sather, A. (2006). Sound, presence, and power: "Student voice" in educational research and reform. *Curriculum Inquiry, 36*(4), 359–380.

Cook-Sather, A. (2010). Students as learners and teachers: Taking responsibility, transforming education, and redefining accountability. *Curriculum Inquiry, 40*(4), 555–575.

Covey, D. (2004). Becoming a literacy leader. *Leadership, 33*(4), 34–35.

Cozby, P.C. (2009). *Methods in behavioral research* (10th ed.). Boston: McGraw Hill.

Creswell, J.W. (2009). *Research design: Qualitative, quantitative, and mixed methods approaches* (3rd ed.). Los Angeles: Sage.

Cummins, J. (1996). *Negotiating identities: Education for empowerment in a diverse society.* Los Angeles: California Association for Bilingual Education.

Darling-Hammond, L., & McLaughlin, M.W. (1995). Policies that support professional development in an era of reform. *Phi Delta Kappan, 76*(8), 597–604.

DeJaeghere, J.G., & Zhang, Y. (2008). Development of intercultural competence among U.S. American teachers: Professional development factors that enhance competence. *Intercultural Education, 19*(3), 255–268.

Department for Education. (2010). DfE Single Equality Scheme 2010. Retrieved March 4, 2011, from http://www.education.gov.uk/schools/pupilsupport/inclusionandlearnersupport/inclusion/equalityanddiversity/a0069463/ses-2010

Dixson, A.D., & Rousseau, C.K. (Eds.). (2006). *Critical race theory in education.* New York: Routledge.

Dudley-Marling, C. (2007). Return of the deficit. *Journal of Educational Controversy, 2.* Retrieved May 22, 2009, from http://www.wce.wwu.edu/Resources/CEP/eJournal/v002n001/a004.shtml

Duncan-Andrade, J. (2007). Gangstas, wankstas, and ridas: Defining, developing, and supporting effective teachers in urban schools. *International Journal of Qualitative Studies in Education, 20*(6), 617–638.

Duncan-Andrade, J.M.R., & Morrell, E. (2008). *The art of critical pedagogy.* New York: Peter Lang.

Durie, M. (1995). Tinorangatiratanga: Self-determination. *He Pukenga Korero, 1*(1), 44–53.

Durie, M. (1998). *Te Mana, Te Kawanatonga: The politics of Maori self-determination.* Auckland, New Zealand: Oxford University Press.

Durie, M. (2002). Universal provision, indigeneity and the Treaty of Waitangi. Paper presented at the Roles and Perspectives in the Law Conference in Honour of Sir Ivor Richardson, Wellington, New Zealand.

El-Haj, T.R. (2003). Practicing for equity from the standpoint of the particular: Exploring the work of one urban teacher network. *Teachers College Record, 105,* 817–845.

Elmore, R., Peterson, P., & McCarthey, S. (1996). *Restructuring in the classroom: Teaching, learning, and school organization.* San Francisco: Jossey-Bass.

Engestrom, Y. (1991). Non Scolae Sed Vitae Discimus: Toward overcoming the encapsulation of school learning. *Learning and Instruction, 1,* 243–259.

Fickel, E. H. (2005). Teachers, tundra, and talking circles: Learning history and culture in an Alaskan native village. *Theory and Research in Social Education, 33*(4), 476–507.

Fillion, B. (1983). Let me see you learn. *Language Arts, 50*(6), 702–710.

Fisher, C., Berliner, D., Filby, N., Marliave, R., Cahen, L., & Dishaw, M. (1981). Teaching behaviours, academic learning time, and student achievement: An overview. *The Journal of Classroom Interactions, 17*(1), 2–15.

Fitzsimons, P., & Smith, G. (2000). Philosophy and indigenous cultural transformation. *Educational Philosophy and Theory, 32*(1), 25–41.

Freire, P. (1972). *Pedagogy of the oppressed*. New York: Continuum.

Freire, P. (1973). *Education for critical consciousness*. New York: Seabury Press.

Freire, P. (1976). *Education and the practice of freedom*. London: Writers and Readers Publishing Cooperative.

Gage, N., & Berliner, D. (1992). *Educational psychology*. Boston: Houghton Mifflin.

Gamoran, A., & Berends, M. (1987). The effects of stratification in secondary schools: Synthesis of survey and ethnographic research. *Review of Educational Research, 57*, 415–435.

Gándara, P., Rumberger, R., Maxwell-Jolly, J., & Callahan, R., (2003). English learners in California schools: Unequal resources, unequal outcomes. *Education Policy Analysis Archives, 11*(36). Retrieved October 28, 2005, from http://epaa.asu.edu/epaa/v11n36/

Garet, M.S., Porter, A.C., Desimone, L.M., Birmann, B.F., & Yoon, K.S. (2001). What makes professional development effective? Results from a national sample of teachers. *American Educational Research Journal, 38*(4), 915–945.

Gay, G. (2010). *Culturally responsive teaching. Theory, research and practice* (2nd ed.). New York: Teachers College Press.

Gillard, J. The Hon. (2008, May 13). *Joint media release: Closing the gap between Indigenous and non-Indigenous Australians*. Ministers' Media Centre. Retrieved March 4, 2011, from www.deewr.gov.au/ministers/gillard/media/releases/pages/article_081030_143929.aspx

Gillborn, D. (2007). Accountability, standards, and race inequity in the United Kingdom: Small steps on the road of progress, or defense of White supremacy? In C. E. Sleeter (Ed.), *Facing accountability in education: Democracy & equity at risk* (pp. 145–158). New York: Teachers College Press.

Gillborn, D. (2008). Coincidence or conspiracy? Whiteness, policy and the persistence of the Black/White achievement gap. *Educational Review, 60*(3), 229–248.

Glynn, T., Berryman, M., & Glynn, V. (2000). *The Rotorua Home and Literacy Project*. A report to Rotorua Energy Charitable Trust and Ministry of Education. Rotorua, New Zealand.

Glynn, T., & Glynn, V. (1986). Shared reading by Cambodian mothers and children learning English as a second language. *International Journal of Disability, Development and Education, 33*(3), 159–172.

Glynn, T., Wearmouth, J., & Berryman, M. (2006). *Supporting students with literacy difficulties: A responsive approach*. Open University Press/McGraw-Hill Education.

Gonzalez, N., Moll, L.C., & Amanti, C. (2005). *Funds of knowledge: Theorizing practices in households, communities, and classrooms*. Mahwah, NJ: Lawrence Erlbaum Associates.

Grant, S., Milfont, T., Herd, R., & Denny, S. (2010). Health and wellbeing of a diverse student population: The Youth 200 surveys of New Zealand secondary school students and their implications for education. In V. Green & S. Cherrington (Eds.), *Delving into diversity: An international exploration of issues of diversity in education* (pp. 185–193). New York: Nova Science Publishers.

Gregory, E. (1996). *Making sense of a new world*. London: Paul Chapman.

Grumet, M.R. (1995). The curriculum: What are the basics and are we teaching them? In J.L. Kincheloe & S.R. Steinberg (Eds.), *Thirteen questions* (2nd ed.) (pp. 15–21). New York: Peter Lang.

Guskey, T.R., & Yoon, K.S. (2009). What works in professional development? *Phi Delta Kappan, 90*(7), 495–500.

Hall, C., & Kidman, J. (2004). *Teaching and learning: Mapping the contextual influences. The International Educational Journal, 5*(3), 331–343.

Hattie, J. A. (1999, August). *Influences on student learning.* Professorial Inaugural Lecture, University of Auckland. Auckland, New Zealand.

Hattie, J.A.C. (2009). *Visible learning: A synthesis of 800+ meta-analyses on achievement.* Oxford: Routledge.

Haviland, D., & Rodriguez-Kiino, D. (2008). Closing the gap: The impact of professional development on faculty attitudes toward culturally responsive pedagogy. *Journal of Hispanic Higher Education, 8,* 197–212.

Haycock, K., & Hanushek, E. A. (2010). An effective teacher in every classroom. *Education Next, 10*(3), 46–52.

Head, G. (2003). Effective collaboration: Deep collaboration as an essential element of the learning process. *Journal of Educational Enquiry, 4*(2), 47–61.

Heshusius, L. (1994). Freeing ourselves from objectivity: Managing subjectivity or turning toward a participatory mode of consciousness? *Educational Researcher, 23*(3), 15–22.

Hill, M. L. (2009). Wounded healing: Forming a storytelling community in hip-hop lit. *Teachers College Record, 111*(1), 248–293.

Holdaway, J., Crul, M., & Roberts, C. (2009). Cross-national comparison of provision and outcomes for the education of the second generation. *Teachers College Record, 111*(6), 1381–1403.

Howard, T. C. (2001). Telling their side of the story: African American students' perceptions of culturally relevant teaching. *The Urban Review, 33*(2), 131–149.

Huck, S.W., & Cormier, W.H. (1996). *Reading statistics and research* (2nd ed.). New York: Harper Collins.

Hynds, A.S. (2007). *Navigating the collaborative dynamic: 'Teachers' collaborating across difference.* Unpublished PhD thesis, Victoria University of Wellington. Wellington, New Zealand.

Jackson, P. W. (1968). *Life in classrooms.* New York: Holt, Rinehart and Winston.

Jennings, L. B., & Smith, C. P. (2002). Examining the role of critical inquiry for transformative practices. *Teachers College Record, 104*(3), 456–81.

Johnston, M. (2007). Unpublished research note: The effect of Te Kotahitanga on success rates in NCEA Level 1. *Research and Knowledge Services.* Wellington: New Zealand Qualifications Authority.

Joyce, B., & Showers, B. (2002). *Student achievement through staff development* (3rd ed.). Alexandria, VA: Association for Supervision and Curriculum Development.

Jung, S., & Stone, S. (2008). Sociodemographic and programmatic moderators of early Head Start: Evidence from the National Head Start Research and Evaluation Project. *Children and Schools, 30*(3), 149–157.

Kalantzis, M., & Cope, B. (1999). Multicultural education: Transforming the mainstream. In S. May (Ed.), *Critical multiculturalism: Rethinking multicultural and antiracist education.* London: Falmer Press.

Kanu, Y. (2007). Increasing school success among Aboriginal students: Culturally responsive curriculum or macrostructural variables affecting schooling? *Diaspora, Indigenous, and Minority Education, 1*(1), 21–41.

Kincheloe, J., & Steinberg, S. (1997). *Changing multiculturalism.* Buckingham, England: Open University Press.

Kline, R.B. (2009). *Becoming a behavioral science researcher: A guide to producing research that matters*. New York: Guilford.

Kukutai, T. (2003). The dynamics of ethnicity reporting: Māori in New Zealand—A discussion paper prepared for Te PuniKōkiri. Wellington, New Zealand: Te PuniKōkiri.

Kumar, S. (2010). *Inclusive classroom, social inclusion/exclusion, and diversity: Perspectives, policies and practices*. Delhi, India: Deshkal Publication.

Ladson-Billings, G. (1994). *The dreamkeepers*. San Francisco: Jossey-Bass.

Ladson-Billings, G. (1995). Toward a theory of culturally relevant pedagogy. *American Educational Research Journal, 47*(3), 465–491.

Ladson-Billings, G., & Tate, W.F. (1995). Toward a critical race theory of education. *Teachers College Record, 97*(1), 47–68.

Lee, C.D. (1995). A culturally based cognitive apprenticeship: Teaching African American high school students' skills in literary interpretation. *Reading Research Quarterly, 30*(4), 608–630.

Lee, C.D. (2001). Is October Brown Chinese: A cultural modeling activity system for under-achieving students. *American Educational Research Journal, 38*(1), 97–142.

Lee, C.D. (2006). "Every good-bye ain't gone": Analyzing the cultural underpinnings of class-room talk. *International Journal of Qualitative Studies in Education, 19*(3), 305–327.

Leithwood, K.A., Seashore Louis, K., Anderson, S., & Wahlstrom, K. (2004). *How leadership influences student learning*. New York: Wallace Foundation. Retrieved September14, 2005, from www.wallacefoundation.org

Liégeois, J.P. (2007). Roma education and public policy. *European Education, 39*(1), 11–31.

Lipka, J., & Adams, B. (2004). *Culturally based mathematics education as a way to improve Alaska Native students' math performance*. Appalachian Collaborative Center for Learning, Assessment, and Instruction in Mathematics. Retrieved December 27, 2010, from http://www.uaf.edu/mcc/award-recognition-and-oth/

Lipka, J., Hogan, M.P., Webster, J.P., Yanez, E., Adams, B., Clark, S., & Lacy, D. (2005). Math in a cultural context: Two case studies of a successful culturally-based math project. *Anthropology & Education Quarterly, 36*(4), 367–385.

Little, J.W. (1993). Teachers' professional development in a climate of educational reform. *Educational Evaluation & Policy Analysis, 15*(2), 129–151.

Luciak, M. (2006). Minority schooling and intercultural education: A comparison of recent developments in the old and new EU member states. *Intercultural Education, 17*(1), 73–80.

Macey, E., Decker, J., & Eckes, S. (2009). The Knowledge Is Power Program (KIPP): An analy-sis of one model's efforts to promote achievement in underserved communities. *Journal of School Choice, 3*, 212–241.

Marks, G.N., Cresswell, J., & Ainley, J. (2006). Explaining socioeconomic inequalities in student achievement: The role of home and school factors. *Educational Research and Evaluation, 12*(2), 105–128.

Martin, A.M., & Hand, B. (2009). Factors affecting the implementation of argument in the elementary science classroom: A longitudinal case study. *Research in Science Education, 39*, 17–38.

Matthews, L.E. (2003). Babies overboard! The complexities of incorporating culturally relevant teaching into mathematics instruction. *Educational Studies in Mathematics, 53*, 61–82.

McMillan, J.H. (1996). *Educational research: Fundamentals for the consumer* (2nd ed.). New York: Harper Collins.

McNaughton, S. (2002). *Meeting of minds*. Wellington, New Zealand: Learning Media.

Mehan, H., Hubbard, L., & Datnow, A. (2010). A co-construction perspective on organizational change and educational reform. *Yearbook of the National Society for the Study of Education, 109*(1), 98–112.

Metge, J. (1990). Te rito o teharakeke: Conceptions of the whanau. *Journal of the Polynesian Society, 99*(1) 55–91.

Meyer, L.H., & Evans, I.M. (1993). Science and practice in behavioral intervention: Meaningful outcomes, research validity, and usable knowledge. *Journal of the Association for Persons with Severe Handicaps, 18*, 224–234.

Meyer, L.H., Penetito, W., Hynds, A., Savage, C., Hindle, R., & Sleeter, C.E. (2010). *Evaluation of TeKotahitanga: 2004–2008.* Wellington: New Zealand Ministry of Education. Retrieved May 4, 2011, from http://www.educationcounts.govt.nz/78910

Miller, D., & Macintosh, R. (1999). Promoting resilience in urban African American adolescents: Racial socialization and identity as protective factors. *Social Work Research, 3*, 159–169.

Ministry of Education. (1988). *Tomorrow's schools*. Wellington, New Zealand: Ministry of Education.

Ministry of Education. (2006). *Ngahaeatamatauranga: Annual report on Māori education*. Wellington, New Zealand: Ministry of Education.

Ministry of Education. (2007). *Developing the second Māori education strategy*. Wellington, New Zealand: Ministry of Education.

Ministry of Education. (2009). *Statement of intent: 2009–2014*. Retrieved March 2, 2010, from http://www.minedu.govt.nz/theMinistry/PublicationsAndResrouces/StatementOfIntent/SOI2009.aspx

Ministry of Education. (2010). *Education counts: Teaching staff*. Retrieved February 15, 2011, from http://www.educationcounts.govt.nz/statistics/schooling/ts/teaching_staff

Moll, L. (1988). Some key issues in teaching Latino students. *Language Arts, 65*(5), 465–472.

Moll, L. (1992). Bilingual classroom studies and community analysis: Some recent trends. *Educational Researcher, 21*, 20–24.

Moll, L.C., & González, N. (1994). Lessons from research with language-minority children. *Journal of Reading Behavior, 26*(4), 439–456.

Moll, L., & Ruiz, R. (2002). The schooling of Latino students. In M. Suarez-Orozco & M. Paez (Eds.), *Contexts for learning: Sociocultural dynamics in children's development* (pp. 19–42). New York: Oxford University Press.

Moore, D., Anderson, A., Timperly, H., Glynn, T., Macfarlane, A., Brown, D., & Thomson, C. (1999). *Caught between stories: Special education in New Zealand*. Wellington: New Zealand Council for Education Research.

Morrison, K.A., Robbins, H.H., & Rose, D.G. (2008). Operationalizing culturally relevant pedagogy: A synthesis of classroom-based research. *Equity & Excellence in Education, 41*(4), 433–435.

Moyle, D. (2005). Quality educators produce quality outcomes: Some thoughts on what this means in the context of teaching Aboriginal and Torres Strait Islander students in Australia's public education system. *Primary & Middle Years Educator, 3*(2), 11–14.

Nathan, R.P. (2007). How should we read the evidence about Head Start? Three views. *Journal of Policy Analysis and Management, 26*, 673–689.

Neufield, B., & Roper, D. (2003). *Coaching: A strategy for developing instructional capacity.* Washington, DC: The Aspen Institute Program on Education and the Annenberg Institute for School Reform.

Nieto, S. (2000). *Affirming diversity: The sociopolitical context of multicultural education* (3rd ed.). New York: Longman.

Noguera, P. (2002). Understanding the link between race and academic achievement and creating schools where that link can be broken. *SAGE Race Relations Abstracts, 27*(3), 5–15.

Nykiel-Herbert, B. (2010). Iraqi refugee students: From a collection of aliens to a community of learners. *Multicultural Education, 17*(30), 2–14.

Oakes, J. (1985). *Keeping track: How schools structure inequality.* New Haven, CT: Yale University Press.

O'Connor, C. (1997). Dispositions toward (collective) struggle and educational resilience in the inner city: A case analysis of six African-American high school students. *American Educational Research Journal, 34*(4), 593–629.

Oliver, E., de Botton, L., Soler, M., & Merrill, B. (2011). Cultural intelligence to overcome educational exclusion. *Qualitative Inquiry, 17*(3), 267–276.

Payne, R.K. (2009). Using the lens of economic class to help teachers understand and teach students from poverty: A response. *Teachers College Record*, Date Published: May 17, 2009. Retrieved February 14, 2011, from http://www.tcrecord.org ID Number: 15629.

Penetito, W. (2001). *If we only knew . . . Contextualising Māori knowledge. Early childhood education for a democratic society.* Wellington: New Zealand Council for Educational Research.

Penetito, W. (2010). *What's Māori about Māori education?* Wellington, New Zealand: Victoria University Press.

Pere, R. (1994). *Ako: Concepts and learning in the Māori tradition.* Wellington, New Zealand: Te Kōhanga Reo.

Pershey, M.G. (2010). A comparison of African American students' self-perceptions of school competence with their performance on state-mandated achievement tests and normed tests of oral and written language and reading. *Preventing School Failure, 55*(1), 53–62.

Pihama, L., Cram, F., & Walker, S. (2002). Creating methodological space: A literature review of Kaupapa Maori research. *Canadian Journal of Native Education, 26*, 30–43.

Poplin, M., & Weeres, J. (1992). *Voices from the inside: A report on schooling from inside the classroom.* Claremont, CA: Claremont Graduate School, Institute for Education in Transformation.

Ravitch, D. (2010). *The death and life of the great American school system: How testing and choice are undermining education.* New York: Basic Books.

Rist, R. (1970). Student social class and teacher expectations: The self-fulfilling prophecy in ghetto education. *Harvard Educational Review, 70*, 257–301.

Robinson, V. (2007). *Student leadership and student outcomes: Identifying what works and why.* ACEL Monograph Series. Victoria: Australian Council for Educational Leaders.

Robinson, V., Lloyd, C., & Rowe, K. (2007). The impact of leadership on student outcomes: An analysis of the differential effects of leadership types. *Educational Administration Quarterly*, 44(5), 635–674.

Rodríguez Izquierdo, R.M. (2009). La investigación sobre la educación intercultural en España, *Archivos Analíticos de Políticas Educativas*, 17(4). Retrieved February 16, 2011, from http://epaa.asu.edu/epaa/

Rogoff, B. (1990). *Apprenticeship in thinking: Cognitive development in social context*. New York: Oxford University Press.

Sanders, M. G. (1997). Overcoming obstacles: Academic achievement as a response to racism and discrimination. *Journal of Negro Education*, 66(1), 83–93.

Savage, C., Hindle, R., Meyer, L.H., Hynds, A., Penetito, W., & Sleeter, C.E. (2011). Culturally responsive pedagogies in the classroom: Indigenous student experiences across the curriculum. *Asia-Pacific Journal of Teacher Education*, 39(3), 183–198.

Shadish, W.R., Cook, T.D., & Campbell, D.T. (2001). *Experimental and quasi-experimental designs for generalized causal inference*. New York: Houghton Mifflin.

Shields, C., Bishop, R., & Mazawi, A.E. (2005). *Pathologizing practices: The impact of deficit thinking on education*. New York: Peter Lang.

Sidorkin, A.M. (2002). *Learning relations*. New York: Peter Lang.

Simon, J., & Smith, L.T. (Eds.). (2001). *A civilising mission? Perceptions and representations of the New Zealand Native Schools System*. Auckland, New Zealand: Auckland University Press.

Sleeter, C.E. (2009). Developing teacher epistemological sophistication about multicultural curriculum: A case study. *Action in Teacher Education*, 31(1), 3–13.

Sleeter, C.E., & Montecinos, C. (1999). Forging partnerships for multicultural education. In S. May (Ed.), *Critical multiculturalism: Rethinking multicultural and anti-racist education* (pp. 113–137). London: Falmer Press.

Sleeter, C.E., & Stillman, J. (2007). Navigating accountability pressures. In C.E. Sleeter (Ed.), *Facing accountability in education: Democracy & equity at risk* (pp. 13–29). New York: Teachers College Press.

Smith, G.H. (1992). *Tane-nu i-a-rangi's legacy. . . propping up the sky: KaupapaMāori as resistance and intervention*. Paper presented at the New Zealand Association for Research in Education/Australia Association for Research in Education joint conference. Deakin University, Australia.

Smith, G.H. (1997). *Kaupapa Māori as transformative praxis*. Unpublished PhD thesis, University of Auckland, Auckland, New Zealand.

Smith, L.T. (1999). *Decolonising methodologies: Research and indigenous people*. London/ Dunedin: Zed Books/University of Otago Press.

Snow-Runner, R., & Lauer, P.A. (2005). *Professional development analysis*. Denver, CO: Midcontinent Research for Education and Learning.

Solórzano, D.G., & Delgado Bernal, D. (2001). Examining transformational resistance through a critical race and LatCrit theory framework: Chicana and Chicano students in an urban context. *Urban Education*, 36(3), 308–342.

Steckler, A., & McLeroy, K.R. (2008). Editorial: The importance of external validity. *American Journal of Public Health*, 98, 9–10.

Storz, M.G. (2008). Educational inequity from the perspectives of those who live it: Urban middle school students' perspectives on the quality of their education. *Urban Review*, 40, 247–267.

Stromquist, N. (1992). Women and literacy: Promises and constraints. *Annals of the American Academy of Political & Social Science, 520*, 54–66.

Task Force to Review Educational Administration. (1988). *Administering for excellence* (Picot Report). Wellington, New Zealand: Government Printer.

Tejeda, C., Espinoza, M., & Gutierrez, K. (2003). Toward a decolonizing pedagogy: Social justice reconsidered. In P.P. Trifonas (Ed.), *Pedagogies of difference: Rethinking education for social change* (pp. 10–40). New York: RoutledgeFalmer.

Timperley, H., Phillips, G., & Wiseman, J. (2003). *The sustainability of professional development in literacy—Parts one and two.* Auckland, New Zealand: University of Auckland.

Timperley, H., & Robinson, V. (2002). *Partnership: Focusing the relationship on the task of school improvement.* Wellington: New Zealand Council for Educational Research.

Timperley, H., Wilson, A., Barrar, H., & Fung, J. (2007). *Teacher professional learning and development: Best Evidence Synthesis (BES).* Wellington: New Zealand Ministry of Education. Retrieved February 12, 2011, from http://www.educationcounts.govt.nz/publications/series/2515/15341

U.S. Department of Education, National Center for Education Statistics. (2010). *The condition of education*, Chapter 3. Retrieved February 14, 2011, from http://nces.ed.gov/programs/coe/2010/section4/indicator27.asp

Valenzuela, A. (1999). *Subtractive schooling: U.S.-Mexican youth and the politics of caring.* Albany: State University of New York Press.

Villegas, A.M., & Lucas, T. (2002). *Educating culturally responsive teachers: A coherent approach.* Albany: State University of New York Press.

Vygotsky, L.S. (1978). *Mind in society: The development of higher psychological processes.* London: Harvard University Press.

Wagstaff, L., & Fusarelli, L. (1995). Establishing, collaborative governance and leadership. In P. Reyes, J. Scribner, & A. Scribner (Eds.), *Lessons from high-performing Hispanic schools: Creating learning communities* (pp. 19–35). New York: Teachers College Press.

Widdowson, D., Dixon, R., & Moore, D. (1996). The effects of teacher modeling of silent reading on students' engagement during Sustained Silent Reading. *Educational Psychology, 16*, 171–180.

Wilson, B.L., & Corbett, H.D. (2001). *Listening to urban kids: School reform and the teachers they want.* Albany: State University of New York Press.

Wilson, S.M., & Berne, J. (1999). Teacher learning and the acquisition of professional knowledge: An examination of research on contemporary professional development. *Review of Research in Education, 24*, 173–209.

Woodson, C.G. (1933). *The mis-education of the Negro.* Trenton, NJ: First Africa World Press.

Woolfolk, A. (2001). *Educational psychology* (8th ed.). Needham Heights, MA: Allyn & Bacon.

Yoon, K.S., Duncan, T., Lee, S.W.Y., Scarloss, B., & Shapley, K. (2007). *Reviewing the evidence on how teacher professional development affects student achievement* (Issues & Answers Report, REL 2007–No. 033). Washington, DC: U.S. Department of Education, Institute of Education Sciences, National Center for Education Evaluation and Regional Assistance, Regional Educational Laboratory Southwest. Retrieved February 1, 2011, from http://ies.ed.gov/ncee/edlabs

Yosso, T. (2005). Whose culture has capital? A critical race theory discussion of community cultural wealth. *Race Ethnicity and Education*, 8(1), 69–81.

Young, M. (2004). *Social values of the Daly region: A preliminary assessment. Darwin.* Draft report to the CRG, School for Social and Policy Research, Charles Darwin University, Darwin, Australia.

Ysseldyke, J., & Christenson, S. (1998). *TIES-II, the instructional environment system II: A system to identify a student's instructional needs.* Longmont, CO: Sopris West.

Zozakiewicz, C., & Rodriguez, A. J. (2007). Using sociotransformative constructivism to create multicultural and gender-inclusive classrooms: An intervention project for teacher professional development. *Educational Policy*, 21(2), 397–425.

INDEX

ROCHELLE BROCK &
RICHARD GREGGORY JOHNSON III,
Executive Editors

Black Studies and Critical Thinking is an inter-
disciplinary series which examines the intellectual traditions of and cultural contributions made by people of African descent throughout the world. Whether it is in literature, art, music, science, or academics, these contributions are vast and far-
reaching. As we work to stretch the boundaries of knowledge and understanding of
issues critical to the Black experience, this series offers a unique opportunity to
study the social, economic, and political forces that have shaped the historic experience of Black America, and that continue to determine our future. Black Studies and
Critical Thinking is positioned at the forefront of research on the Black experience,
and is the source for dynamic, innovative, and creative exploration of the most vital
issues facing African Americans. The series invites contributions from all disciplines
but is specially suited for cultural studies, anthropology, history, sociology, literature,
art, and music.

Subjects of interest include (but are not limited to):

- EDUCATION
- SOCIOLOGY
- HISTORY
- MEDIA/COMMUNICATION
- RELIGION/THEOLOGY
- WOMEN'S STUDIES

- POLICY STUDIES
- ADVERTISING
- AFRICAN AMERICAN STUDIES
- POLITICAL SCIENCE
- LGBT STUDIES

For additional information about this series or for the submission of manuscripts,
please contact Dr. Brock (Indiana University Northwest) at brock2@iun.edu or Dr.
Johnson (University of Vermont) at richard.johnson-III@uvm.edu.

To order other books in this series, please contact our Customer Service Department:

(800) 770-LANG (within the U.S.)
(212) 647-7706 (outside the U.S.)
(212) 647-7707 FAX

Or browse online by series at www.peterlang.com.